MICHEL LEGRAND

THE PIANO COLLECTION

Photos on pgs 4 & 5, courtesy of:
Michael Ochs Archives/Getty Images and
Paul Popper/Popperfoto/Getty Images

ISBN: 978-1-78305-142-7

Visit Hal Leonard Online at
www.halleonard.com

Contact us:
Hal Leonard
7777 West Bluemound Road
Milwaukee, WI 53213
Email: info@halleonard.com

In Europe, contact:
Hal Leonard Europe Limited
42 Wigmore Street
Marylebone, London, W1U 2RY
Email: info@halleonardeurope.com

In Australia, contact:
Hal Leonard Australia Pty. Ltd.
4 Lentara Court
Cheltenham, Victoria, 3192 Australia
Email: info@halleonard.com.au

À LA LUMIERE D'UNE ÉTOILE 6

BILBOQUET 9

CHINA DOLL 13

THE HANDS OF TIME (BRIAN'S SONG) 17

HAPPY 20

HOW DO YOU KEEP THE MUSIC PLAYING? 24

I WILL WAIT FOR YOU 29

JAZZ TIME 32

LE CINÉMA 37

LE PARADIS 42

LE ROUGE ET LE NOIR 45

LITTLE BOY LOST (PIECES OF DREAMS) 48

NOBODY KNOWS 52

ONCE UPON A SUMMERTIME 55

ONE AT A TIME 58

PAPA, CAN YOU HEAR ME? 62

SECRET PLACES 66

SWEET GINGERBREAD MAN 69

TELL A LIE 72

WAITING 75

WATCH WHAT HAPPENS 78

WHAT ARE YOU DOING THE REST OF YOUR LIFE? 82

THE WINDMILLS OF YOUR MIND 86

THE YEARS OF MY YOUTH 90

YOU MUST BELIEVE IN SPRING 93

MICHEL LEGRAND

THE PIANO COLLECTION

Michel Legrand is perhaps France's most prolific film & TV composer, songwriter, arranger and pianist. He first came to the notice of Hollywood after the success of Jacques Demy's movie *Les Parapluies de Cherbourg* (1964) an entirely sung romantic drama for which he wrote the music. This film and, to a lesser extent, Demy's follow-up *Les Demoiselles de Rochefort* (1967), were both popular successes and both put Legrand in international demand. His first Hollywood payday was for scoring the original version of *The Thomas Crown Affair* (1968), a movie for which he also co-wrote 'The Windmills Of Your Mind', an ethereal song performed by Noel Harrison. His next American score, for *Summer of '42* (1971), won Legrand an Academy Award.

By this time Legrand had long since made a memorable acting appearance in one of the French New Wave's best films, Agnès Varda's *Cléo de 5 à 7* (1962). He played Bob, a hyperactive pianist and composer who represents one of the suddenly irrelevant forces in the life of pop singer Cléo Victoire who, for the film's duration, is awaiting the results of a potentially grim medical diagnosis.

The son of conductor and composer Raymond Legrand, Michel attended the Paris Conservatoire from the age of eleven until he was eighteen, graduating with top honours both as a composer and a pianist. After graduation his first love was jazz and he threw himself into it enthusiastically, first in New York and then in Paris during the late 1950s, collaborating with Miles Davis and John Coltrane in the US and then joining Gus Wallez and Guy Pedersen back in France. Legrand's 'You Must Believe In Spring', 'What Are You Doing The Rest Of Your Life?' and 'Watch What Happens' (all included here) have become jazz standards. Jazz collaborations

'MICHEL LEGRAND'S CAREER HAS BEEN TIRELESS IN ITS ENERGY AND SCOPE'

have recurred throughout his long career: Ray Brown and Shelley Manne in the late 1960s; Stan Getz and Phil Woods in the 1970s; Stephane Grappelli in the early 1990s.

His appetite for working in different genres is legendary. He has conducted orchestras in Vancouver, Montreal, Atlanta, Pittsburgh, Denver and St Petersburg. He collaborated with everyone from Ray Charles to Perry Como, Kiri Te Kanawa to Barbra Streisand, Aretha Franklin to Shirley Bassey.

To date Legrand's film scores number around 200. A surprise success was 'The Hands Of Time' Legrand's instrumental theme for a 1972 TV biopic movie *Brian's Song*. The picture subsequently got a

theatrical release and Legrand's instrumental version made the charts for eight weeks. *Brian's Song* was remade in 2001, *sans* Legrand, while *The Thomas Crown Affair* got its own remake in 1999 with Sting taking over vocal duties on 'The Windmills Of Your Mind'.

A glance through the titles in this collection reflects the sheer diversity of Legrand's work. Music from several French films is included. There are the jazz standards he wrote as a relatively young man. 'Papa Can You Hear Me?' comes from Barbra Streisand's labour of love *Yentl*. Bringing us up to date are three Legrand songs from *Marguerite*, the latest musical from the creators of *Les Misérables*, Alain Boublil and Claude-Michel Schönberg: 'China Doll', 'Jazz Time' and 'Waiting'.

Michel Legrand's career has been tireless in its energy and scope. Despite the breadth of his musical activities this superb collection reminds us in particular of his love of the piano and his early days as a jazz pianist. His bit part appearance in *Cléo de 5 à 7* remains a useful reminder of those days and of Legrand's youthful aura of energy, impatience and experiment, qualities which, as the decades passed, never left him.

À La Lumiere D'Une Étoile

Words by Claude Nougaro
Music by Michel Legrand

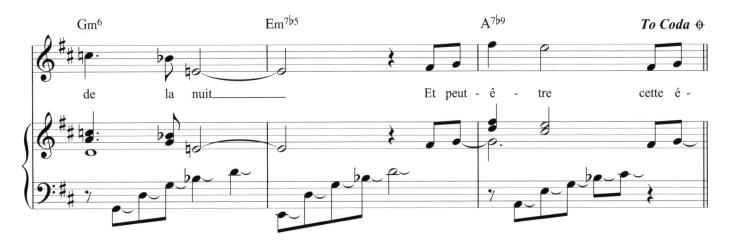

Plus agité

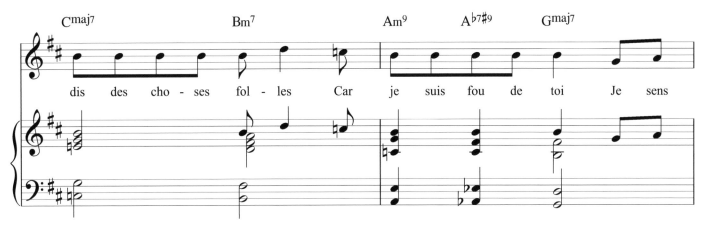

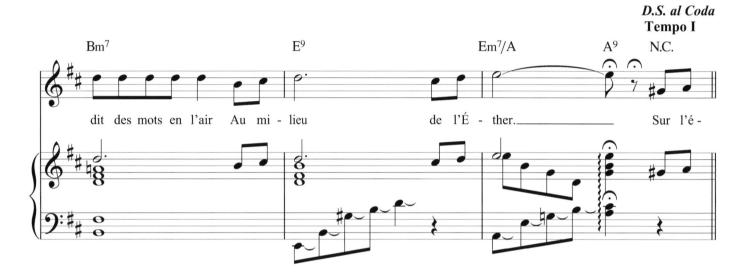

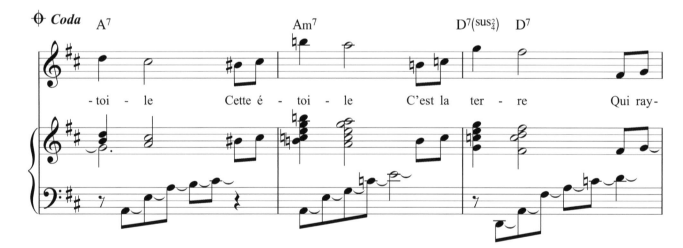

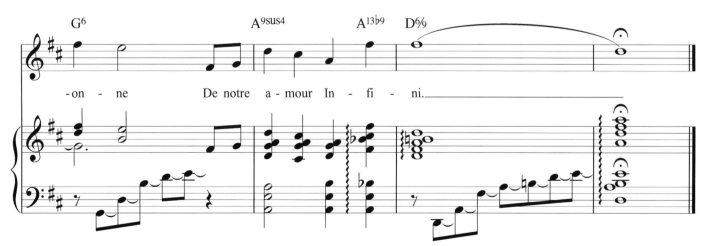

Bilboquet

Words by Claude Nougaro
Music by Michel Legrand

Jazz-valse moderato

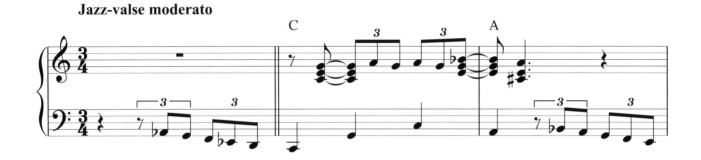

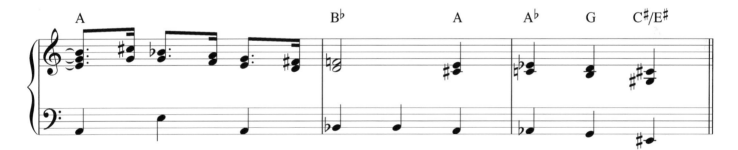

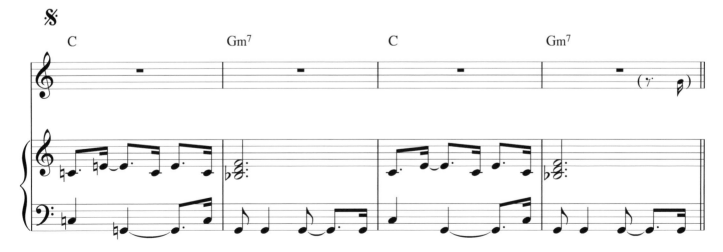

Dans un rêve i - nou - bli - a - ble_ A près je ne sais quel ban - quet Je
Loins des pro - pos dis - cu - ta - bles_ Des po - lé - mi - ques alam - bi - quées J'te

6° To Coda

1, 3, 5.

vis le Bon Dieu et le Diable_ trin - quer
bouffe le foie, la foi, le râble_

2, 4.

ro - quets Je vis le Diable et le Bon Dieu S'rou-

- ler un pa - tin mé - mo - ra - a - ble Dieu ri - ait dans sa bar - be bleue

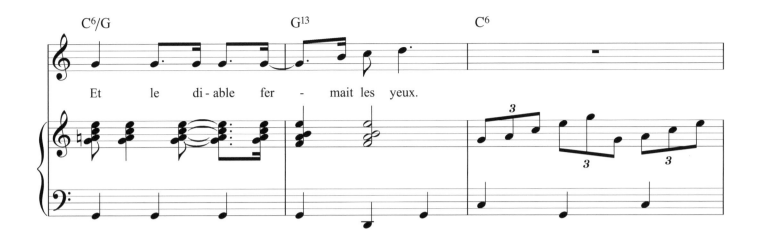

Et le di-able fer - mait les yeux.

D.S. al Coda

Coda

- quet   Rue Saint - Be - noît   à l'heure___ sta - ble   Où

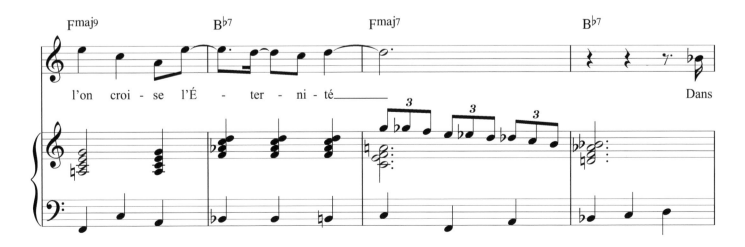

l'on croi - se l'É - ter - ni - té_____   Dans

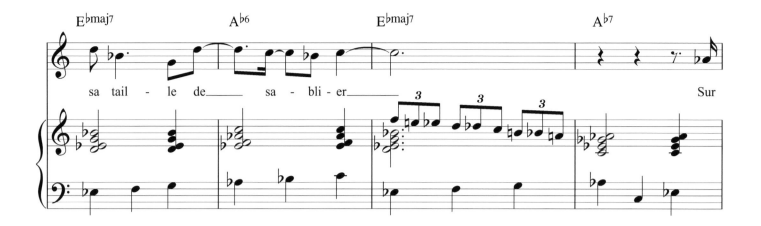

sa tail - le de____ sa - bli - er____ Sur

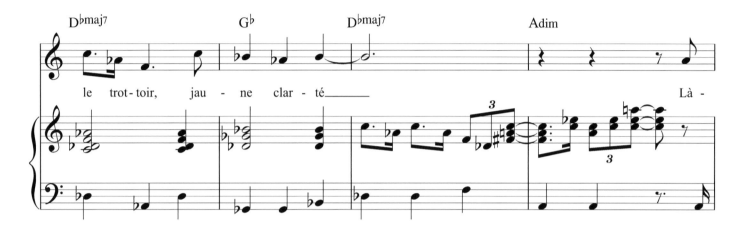

le trot - toir, jau - ne clar - té____ Là -

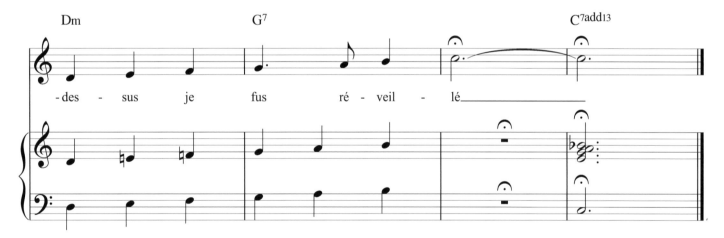

- des - sus je fus ré - veil - lé____

Verse 2:
Si l'on jouait cartes sur table
Fini de traquer, de truquer
Dit le Bon Dieu du mauvais Diable O.K.?
Est-il encore tolérable
De nous vomir, de nous choquer
Et de voir l'homme lamentable casquer?
Là, liquidons le contentieux
Satan, je te trouve adorable.
L'Enfer est mort! Buvons tous deux
Mon eau de vie, ton eau de feu.

Verse 3:
Alors je vis Bon Dieu et Diable
Dans un paraphe gracieux
Signer le parchemin des cieux, équitable.
Puis ils roulèrent sous la table
A grand fracas, dans des hoquets.
Ça se passait au Bilboquet
Rue Saint-Benoît à l'heure stable
Où l'on croise l'Éternité
Dans sa taille de sablier
Sur le trottoir, jaune clarté,
Là-dessus, je fus réveillé.

China Doll

from *Marguerite*

Music by Michel Legrand
Lyrics by Alain Boublil & Herbert Kretzmer

Some-one turns the key, and the chi-na doll stands on tip - toe, pale and pink is she as she pir-ou-ettes to the

F♯m⁷　　　B　　　Em　　　F♯m⁷　　　Em/G　　　Em⁷

mu - sic.　　All　that　she　can　see,　　　as her

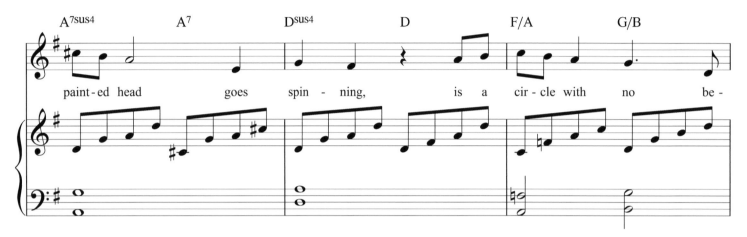

A⁷ˢᵘˢ⁴　　　A⁷　　　Dˢᵘˢ⁴　　　D　　　F/A　　　G/B

paint - ed head　　goes　spin - ning,　　is a　cir - cle with　no　be -

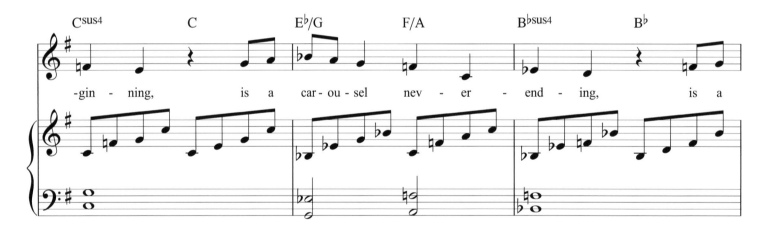

Cˢᵘˢ⁴　　　C　　　E♭/G　　　F/A　　　B♭ˢᵘˢ⁴　　　B♭

-gin - ning,　　is a　car - ou - sel　nev - er - end - ing,　　is a

rall.　　　　　　　　　　　　**a tempo**

Bm⁷♭⁵　　　B⁷♯⁹　B⁷♭⁹　　Em　　　F♯m⁷　　　Em/G　　　Em⁷

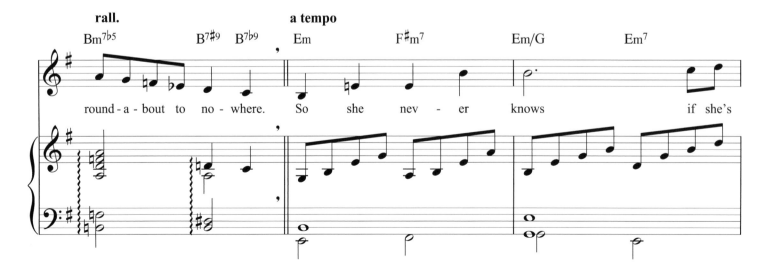

round - a - bout　to　no - where.　So　she　nev - er　knows　　　if she's

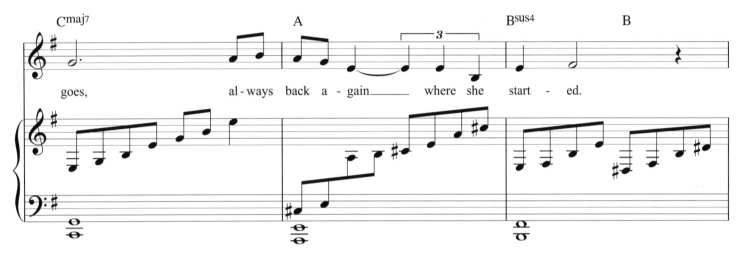

The Hands Of Time

from *Brian's Song (1971)*

Words & Music by Michel Legrand

If the hands of time were hands that I could hold, I'd keep them warm and in my hands they'd not turn cold.

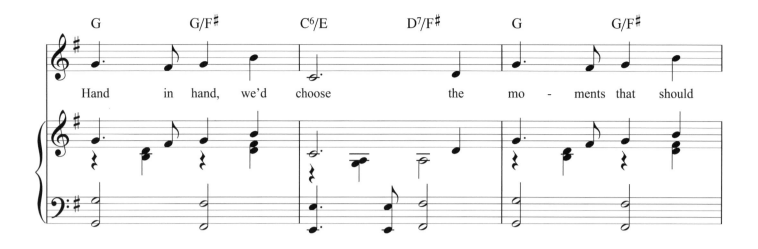

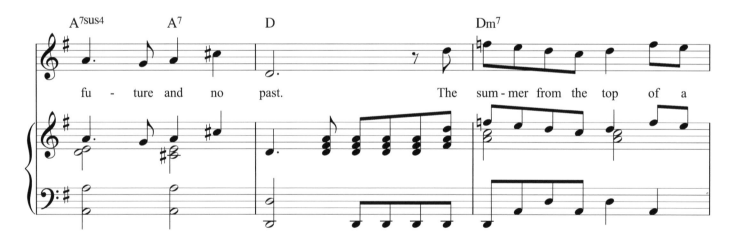

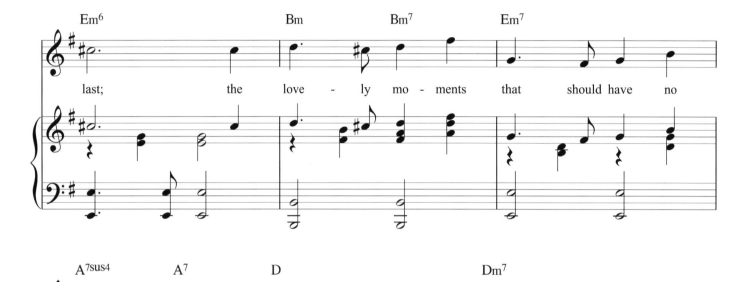

in - no-cence of leaves in the spring. But most of all, the mo - ment when

love first touched me! All the hap - py days would

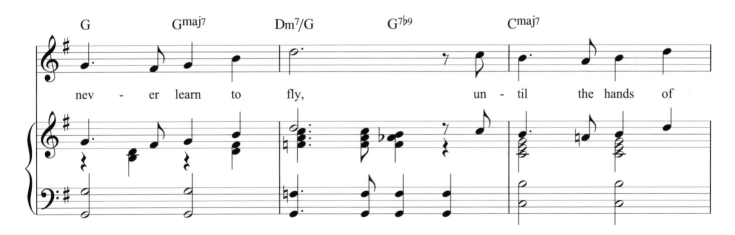

nev - er learn to fly, un - til the hands of

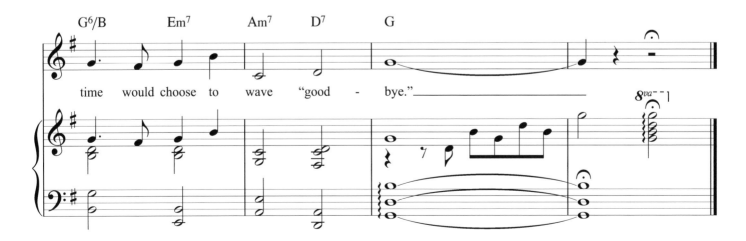

time would choose to wave "good - bye."

Happy

Words by Smokey Robinson
Music by Michel Legrand

Slowly, with feeling

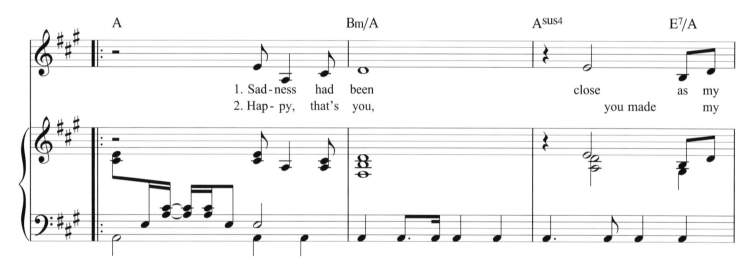

1. Sad-ness had been close as my
2. Hap-py, that's you, you made my

next of kin, then Hap-py came one day,
life brand new. Lost as a lit-tle lamb was I

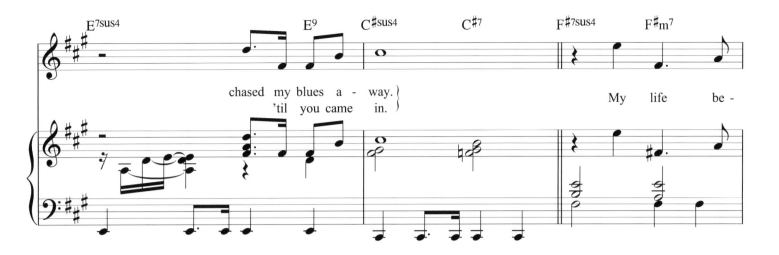

chased my blues a - way. }
'til you came in. }

My life be -

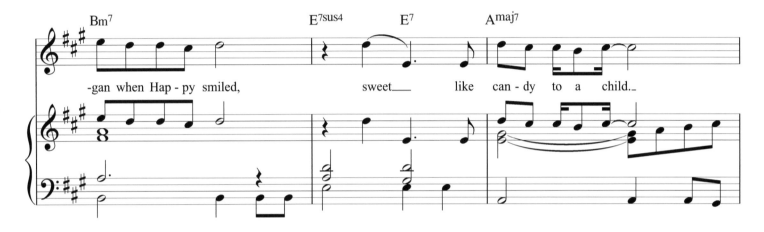

-gan when Hap - py smiled, sweet___ like can - dy to a child.__

Stay here, and love me just a while,___ let

Sad - ness see what Hap - py does, let Hap - py be where Sad - ness was.

Hap - py be where Sad - ness was 'til now.

3. Where have I been?

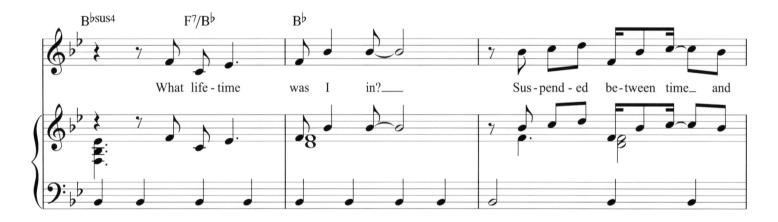

What life - time was I in?___ Sus - pend - ed be - tween time_ and

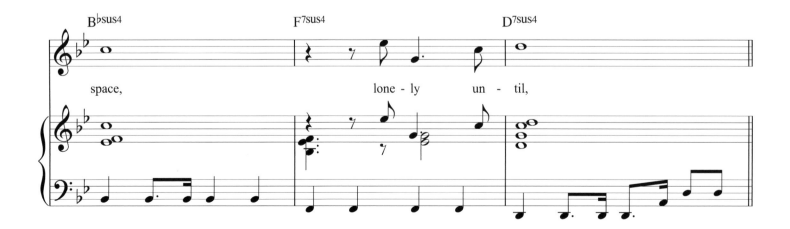

space, lone - ly un - til,

Hap - py came smil - ing up at me,___ Sad - ness had

no choice but to flee.___ I said a prayer___ so si - lent- ly, let

Sad - ness see what Hap - py does, let Hap - py be where Sad - ness was 'til___

a tempo

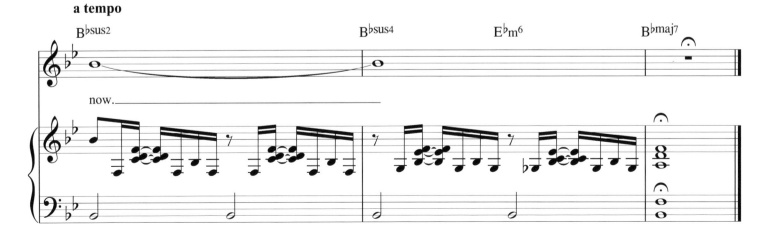

now._____

23

How Do You Keep The Music Playing?

from *Best Friends (1982)*

Words by Alan & Marilyn Bergman
Music by Michel Legrand

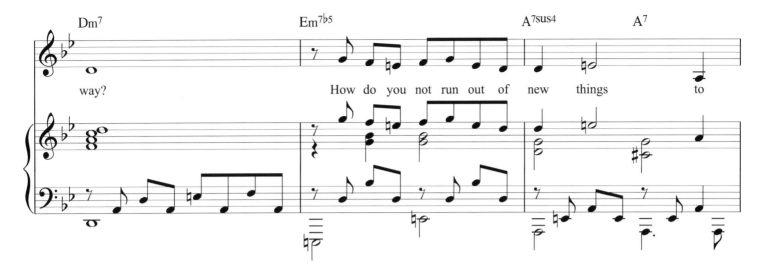

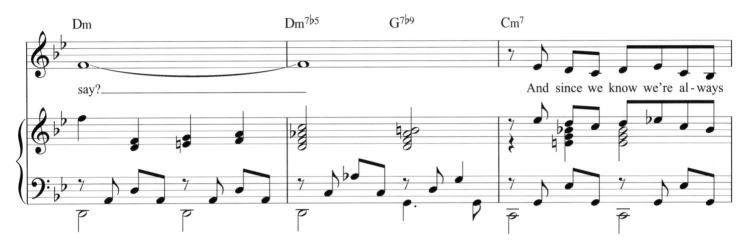

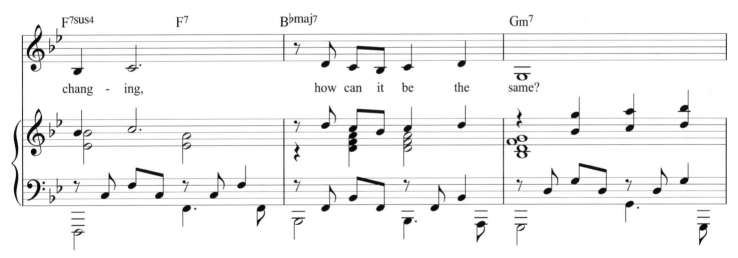

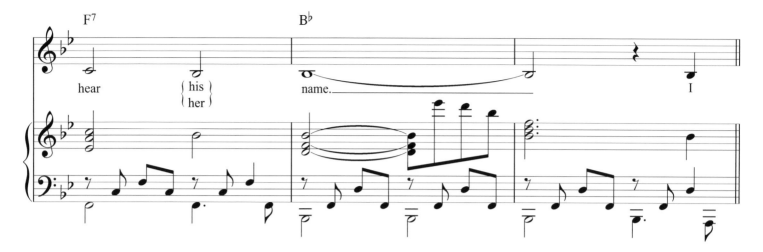

lov - ers,   yet be the best of friends,

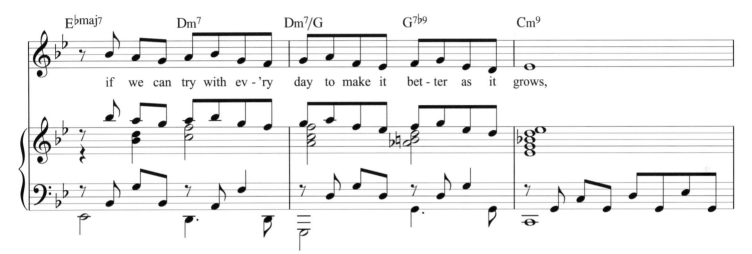

if we can try with ev -'ry day to make it bet - ter as it grows,

with a - ny luck, then I sup - pose_____ the mu - sic nev - er

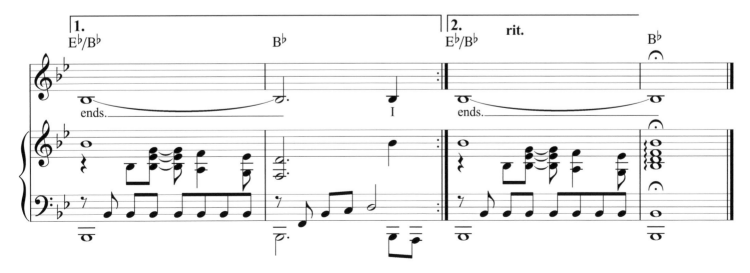

ends._____ I   ends._____

27

Les Parapluies de Cherbourg (1964), by the director Jacques Demy. ZEITGEIST FILMS

I Will Wait For You

from *Les Parapluies de Cherbourg (1964)*

Words by Norman Gimbel
Music by Michel Legrand

Moderate tempo

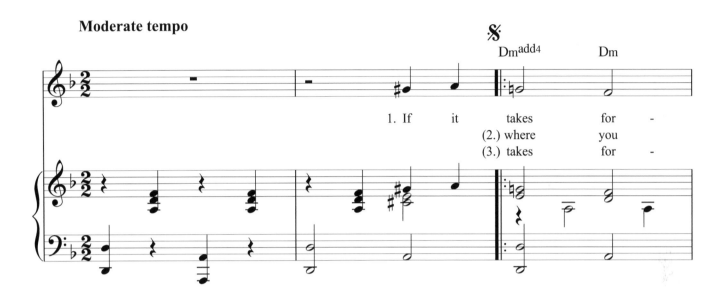

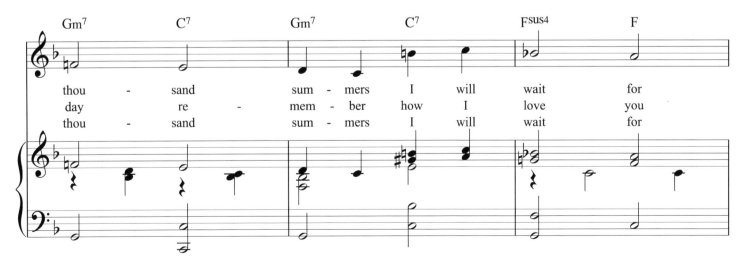

29

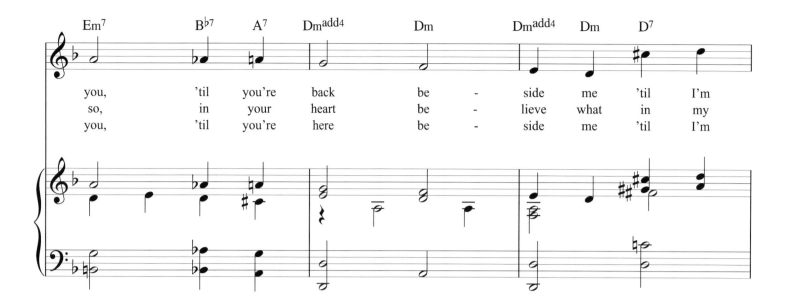

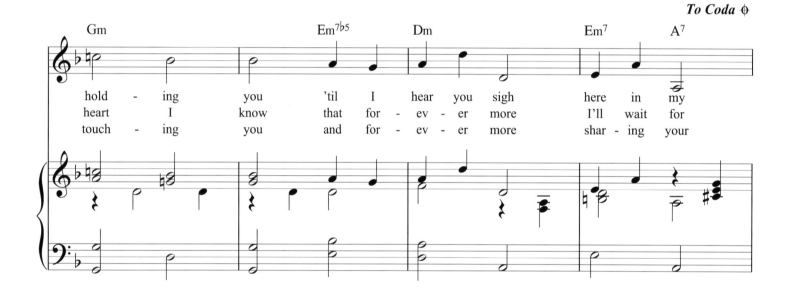

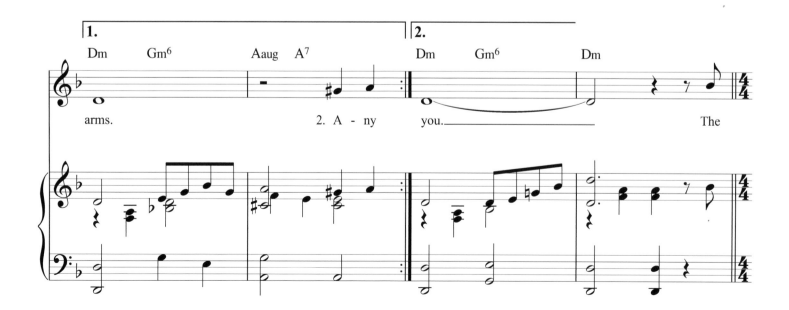

clock will tick a - way the hours one by one___ and then the time will come when all the

wait - ing's done.___ The time when you re - turn and find me here and run,___

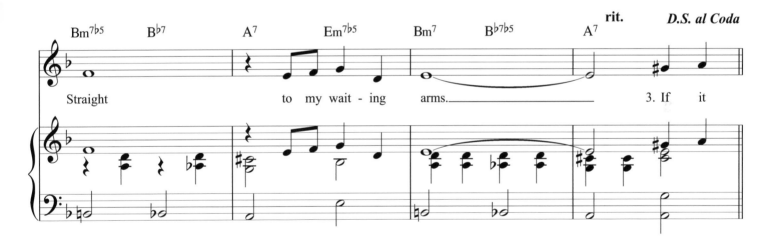

Straight to my wait - ing arms.___ 3. If it

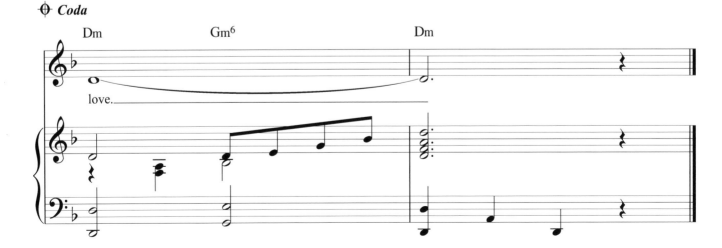

love.___

Jazz Time

from *Marguerite*

Music by Michel Legrand
Lyrics by Alain Boublil & Herbert Kretzmer

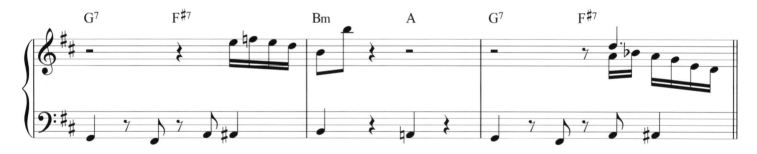

Hit the floor and feel the beat.___ Jazz___ time!

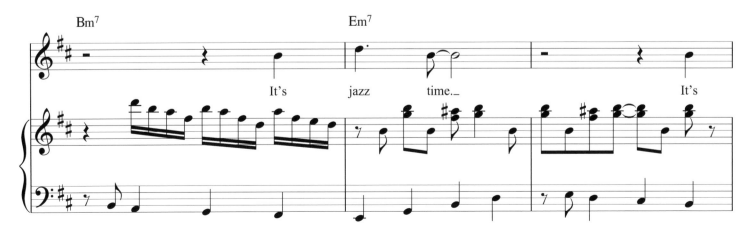

jazz time. Keep hop - pin' till the morn - ing sun!

It's jazz time.

(Jazz time!) It's jazz time. (Jazz time!) No stop - pin'

till the dance is done!

You feel fine and fan-cy-free? You got jazz!

You want fun and com-pa-ny? Now you has! If your

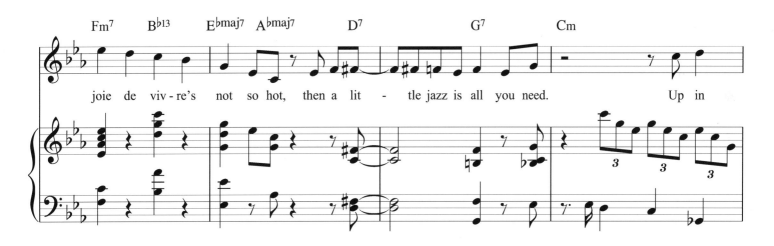

joie de viv-re's not so hot, then a lit - tle jazz is all you need. Up in

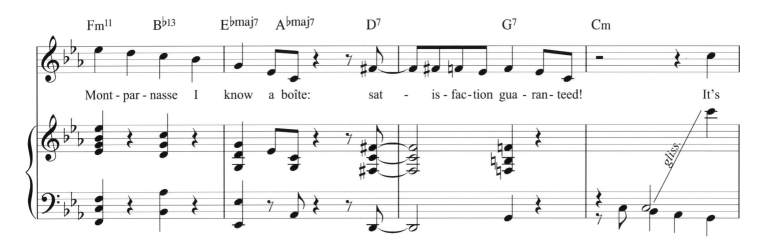

Mont-par-nasse I know a boîte: sat - is-fac-tion gua-ran-teed! It's

jazz   time.___   (Jazz   time!)___   It's   jazz   time.___

(Jazz   time!)___   Keep   hop – pin'   till   the   morn – ing   sun!___

___   It's   jazz   time.   (Jazz   time!)___   It's

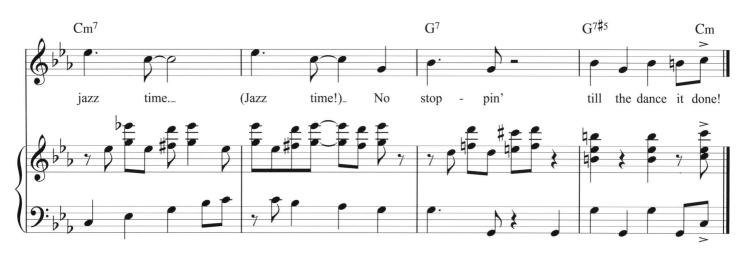

jazz   time.___   (Jazz   time!)___   No   stop – pin'   till   the   dance   it   done!

Le Cinéma

Words by Claude Nougaro
Music by Michel Legrand

1. Sur l'é-cran noir de mes nuits blanches,
2. Sur l'é-cran noir de mes nuits blanches,

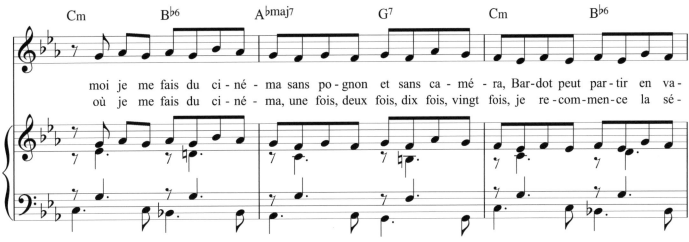

moi je me fais du ci-né - ma sans po-gnon et sans ca - mé-ra, Bar-dot peut par-tir en va-
où je me fais du ci-né - ma, une fois, deux fois, dix fois, vingt fois, je re-com-men-ce la sé-

- cances, ma ve-det-te c'est tou-jours toi
- quence où tu me tom-bes dans les bras...

Pour te dire que je t'ai-me rien à faire, je flanche
Je tour-ne tous les soirs y com-pris le di-manche...

j'ai du cœur mais pas d'es-to-
Par-fois on sonne, j'ou-vre, c'est

-mac c'est pour-quoi je prends ma re-vanche sur l'é-cran noir de mes nuits blanches où je me fais du ci-né-
toi, vais-je te pren-dre par les hanches comme sur l'é-cran de mes nuits

2° To Coda ⊕

Tempo medium

-ma

D'a-bord un gros plan sur tes

38

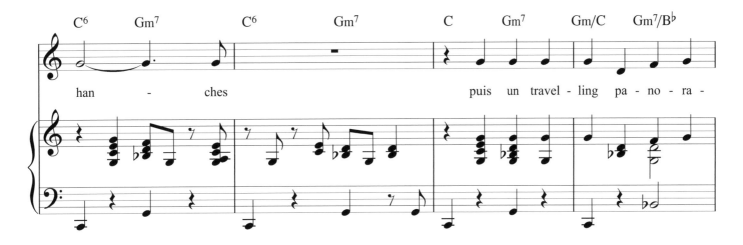

han - ches — puis un travel - ling pa - no - ra -

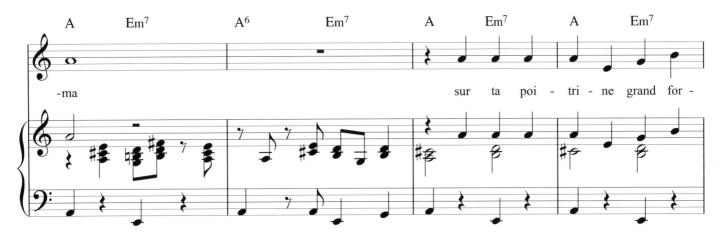

-ma — sur ta poi - tri - ne grand for -

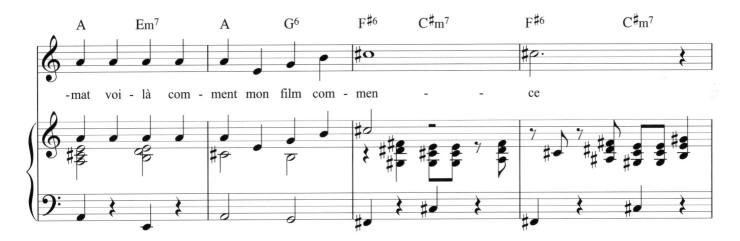

-mat voi - là com - ment mon film com - men - ce

Sou - ri - ant, je m'a - vance vers toi... — Un

Slow-Fox (très rythmé)

mè - tre qua - tre - vingts, des bi - ceps plein les manches je crève l'é - cran de mes nuits

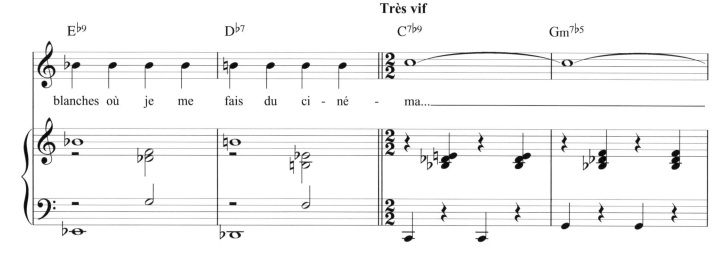

Très vif

blanches où je me fais du ci - né - ma...

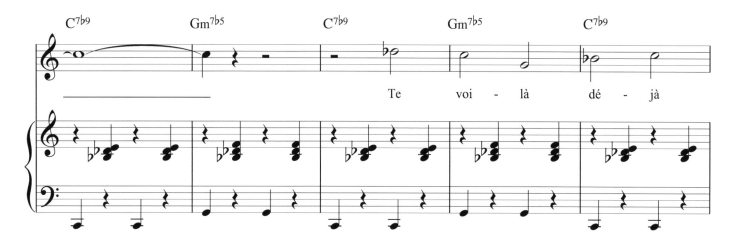

Te voi - là dé - jà

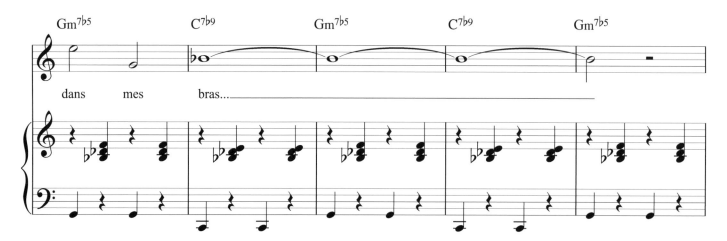

dans mes bras...

40

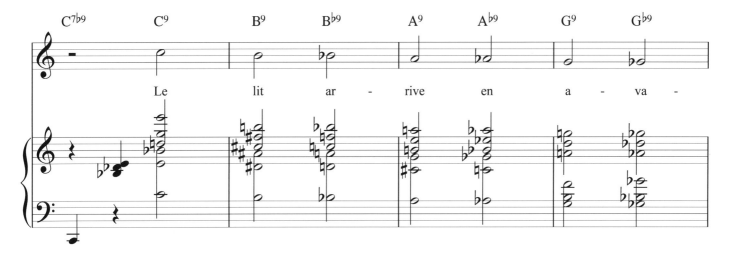

Le lit ar - rive en a - va -

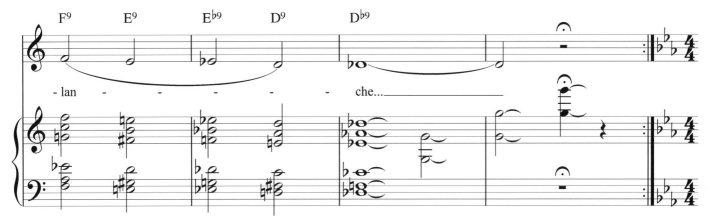

- lan - - - - che...

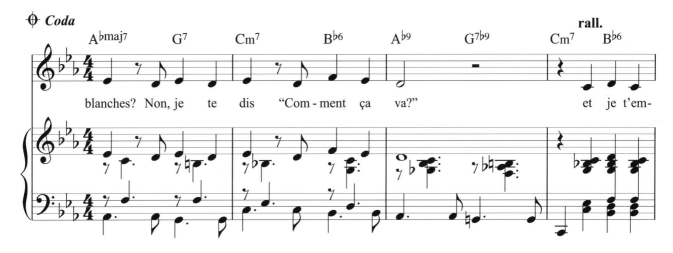

$\oplus$ **Coda**

blanches? Non, je te dis "Com - ment ça va?" et je t'em-

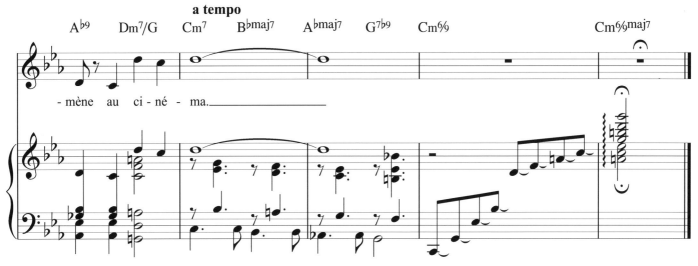

a tempo

- mène au ci - né - ma._____

Le Paradis

Words by Claude Nougaro
Music by Michel Legrand

même u - ne va - lise sous l'o - rage et l'é - clair, mar - chant droit de - vant
même un hô - tel borgne al - lons donc chez le diable! Il n'é - tait pas chez
fond de la mé - moire et des dis - ques de jazz, au pied de no - tre

Plus vite

nous
lui
lit
Ô È - ve, È - ve mon pe - tit te sou - viens - tu

1, 2.

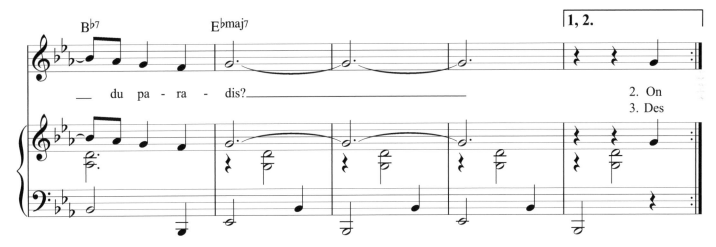

_ du pa - ra - dis?

2. On
3. Des

Slow tempo

3.

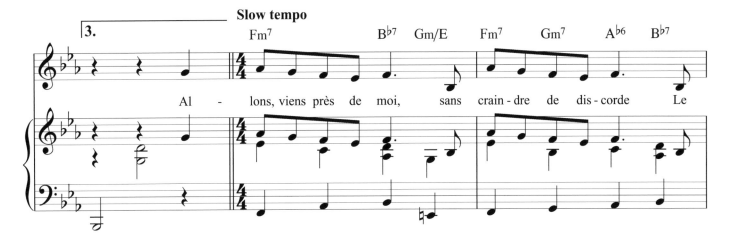

Al - lons, viens près de moi, sans crain - dre de dis - corde Le

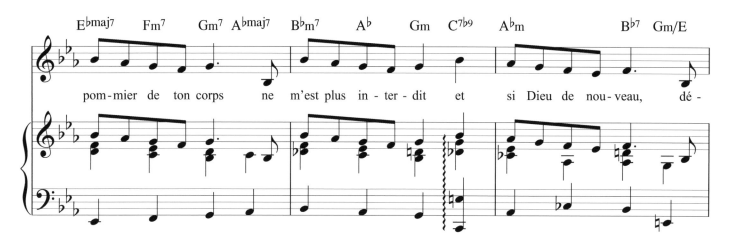

pom - mier de ton corps ne m'est plus in - ter - dit et si Dieu de nou - veau, dé -

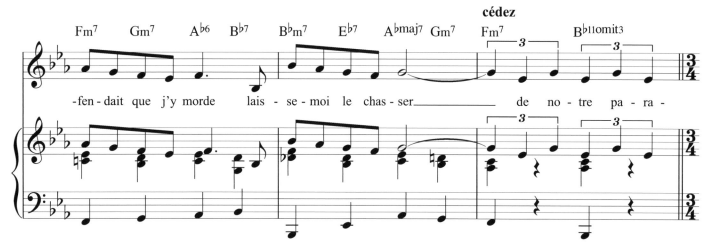

cédez

-fen - dait que j'y morde lais - se - moi le chas - ser_____ de no - tre pa - ra -

Plus vite

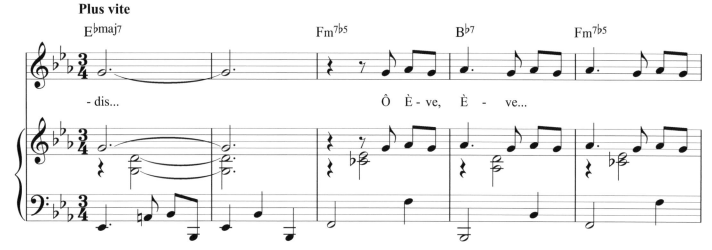

- dis... Ô È - ve, È - ve...

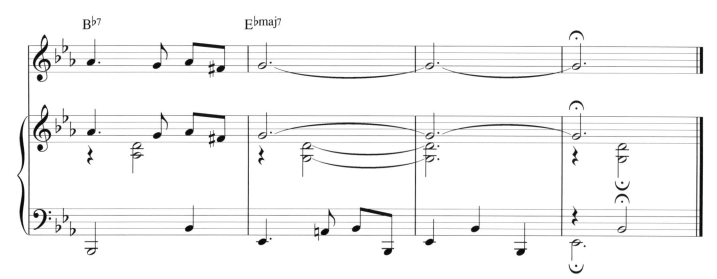

Le Rouge Et Le Noir

Words by Claude Nougaro
Music by Michel Legrand

type noir a - vec une fille rouge en robe de soie noire. L'en -
soie noire au ry - thme d'un blues qui sort du bouge noir. L'en -

-seigne au né - on__ à l'en - trée du bouge é - claire la
-seigne au né - on__ à l'en - trée du bouge bat comme un

chambre noire d'u - ne lu - eur rouge cou - leur d'a - bat - toir et dans cette
cœur noir, l' type se fait tendre, rouge, la fille dit "Non" noir "Qu'est-ce qui te

2° To Coda ⊕

chambre rouge y a le grand type noir qui boit du gin rouge comme un en -
prend?" rouge lui de - mande le noir qui voit sou -

46

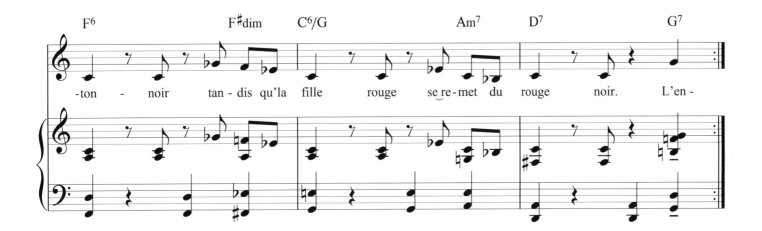

-ton — noir tan-dis qu'la fille rouge se re-met du rouge noir. L'en-

Coda

- dain rouge   "C'est parce que j' suis noir?

—Non, dit la fille rouge c'est parce que

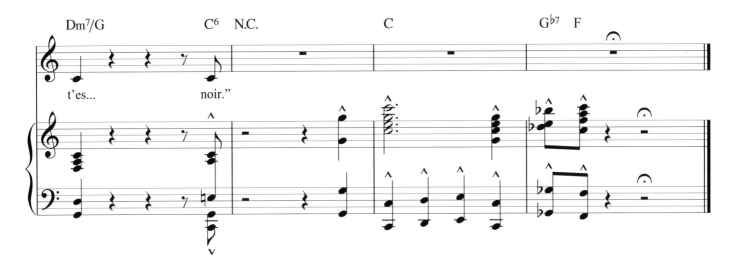

t'es... noir."

Little Boy Lost
(Pieces Of Dreams)

Words by Alan Bergman & Marilyn Bergman
Music by Michel Legrand

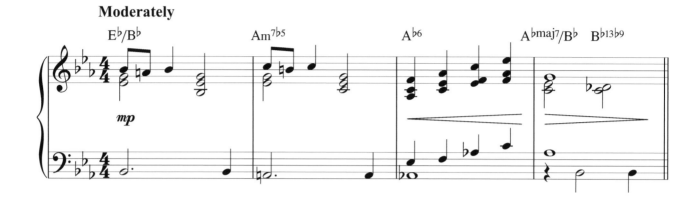

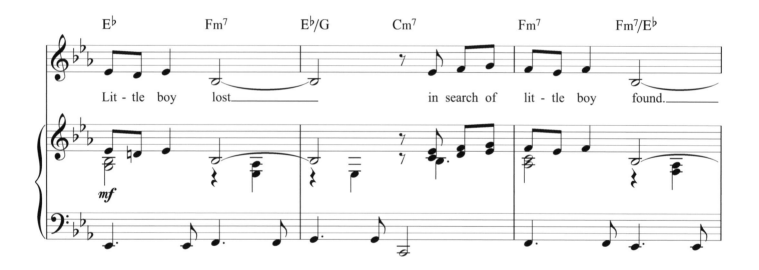

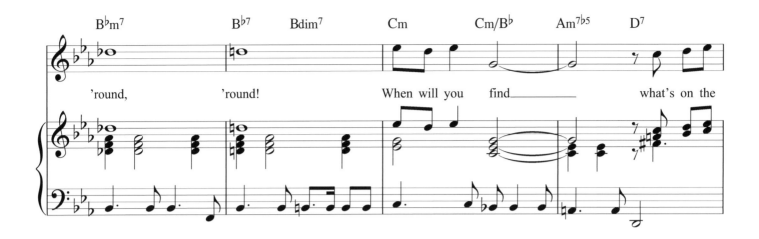

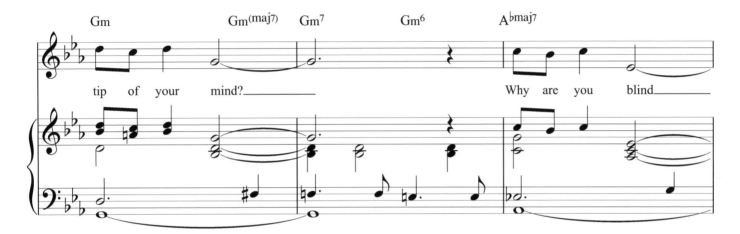

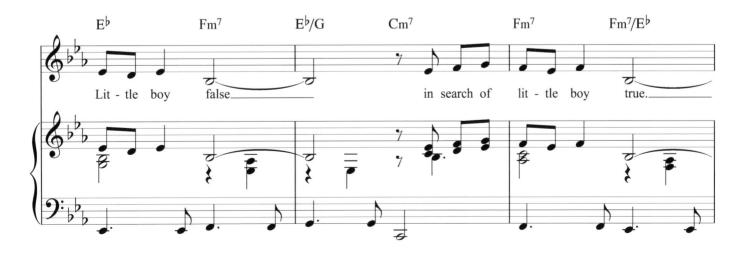

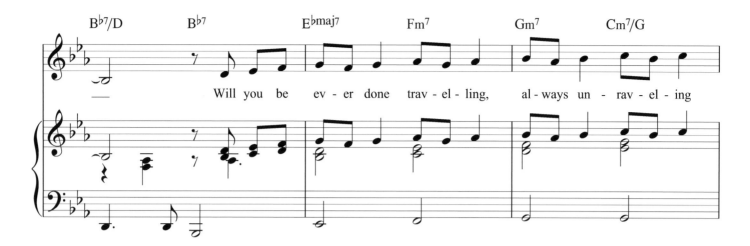

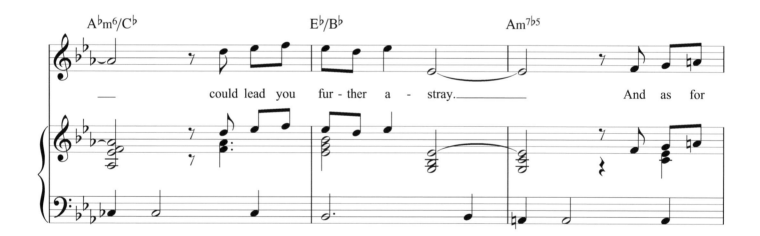

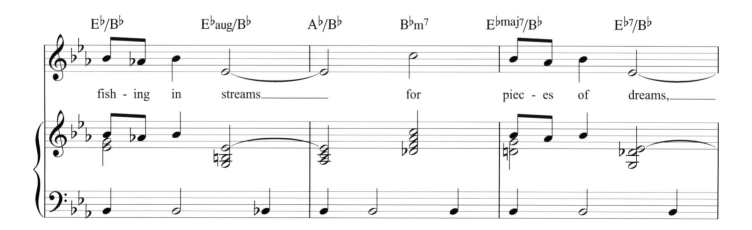

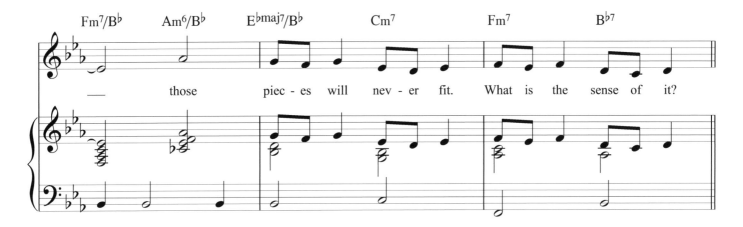

those piec-es will nev-er fit. What is the sense of it?

Lit - tle boy blue,_____ don't let your lit - tle sheep roam._____
(Opt. 2°) Lit - tle boy lost,_____ the woods are run - ning with streams._____

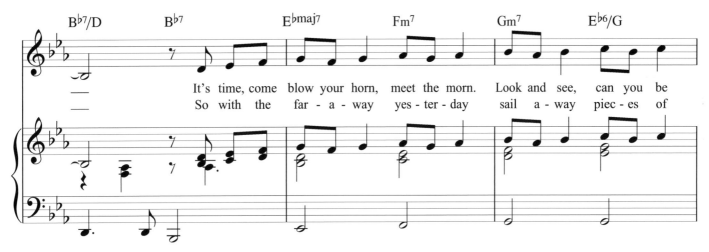

It's time, come blow your horn, meet the morn. Look and see, can you be
So with the far - a - way yes - ter - day sail a - way piec - es of

rit.

far from home?_____
long - - lost dreams._____

dim.

51

Nobody Knows

Music by Michel Legrand
Words by Alan & Marilyn Bergman

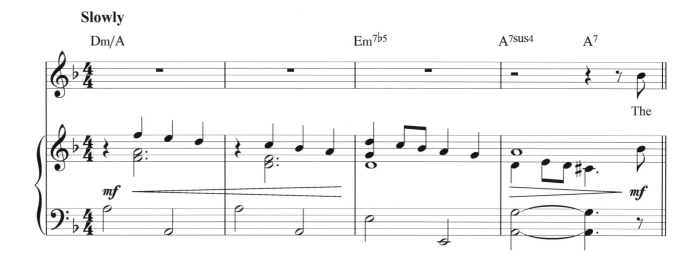

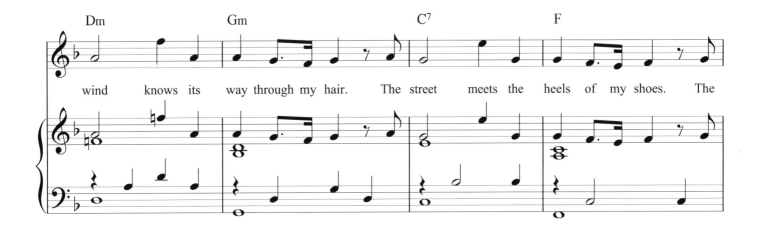

wind knows its way through my hair. The street meets the heels of my shoes. The

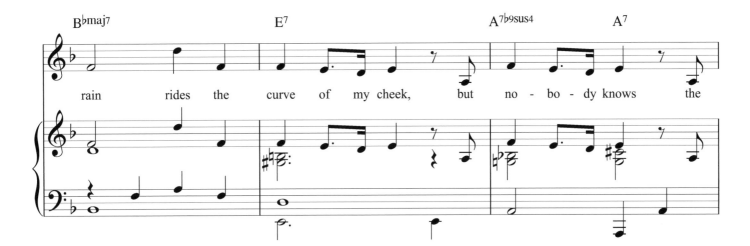

rain rides the curve of my cheek, but no - bo - dy knows the

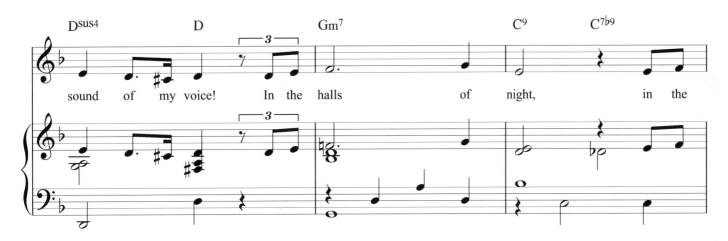

sound of my voice! In the halls of night, in the

caves of day, on the map of time, it's all a

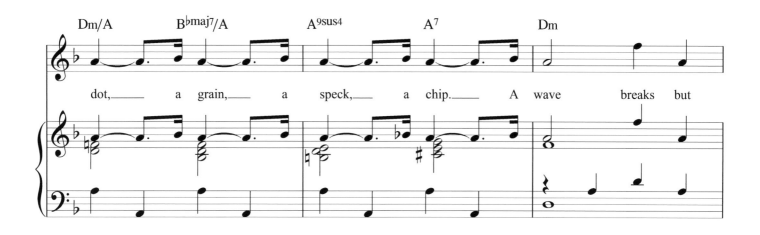

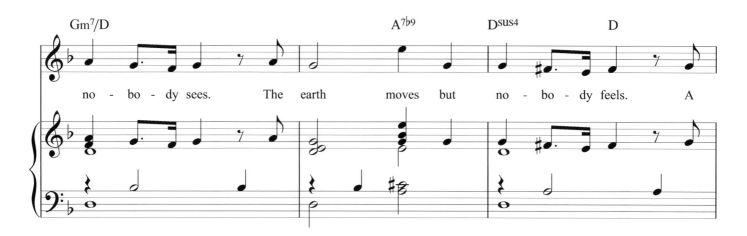

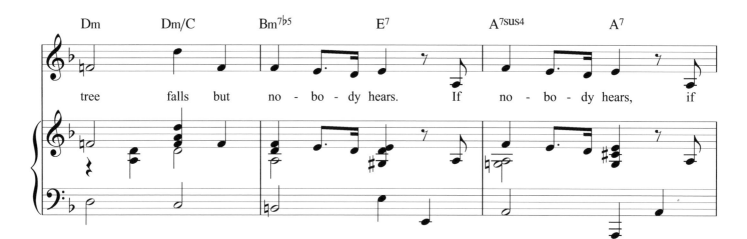

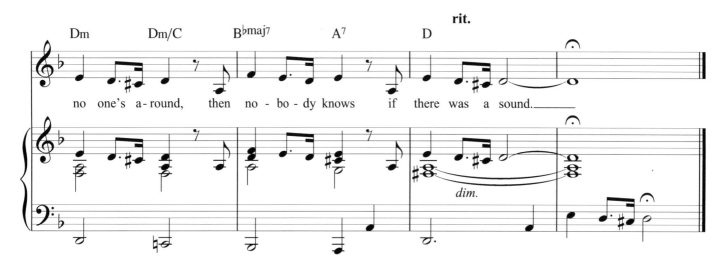

Once Upon A Summertime

Words by Eddy Marnay
Music by Michel Legrand & Eddie Barclay
Translated by Johnny Mercer

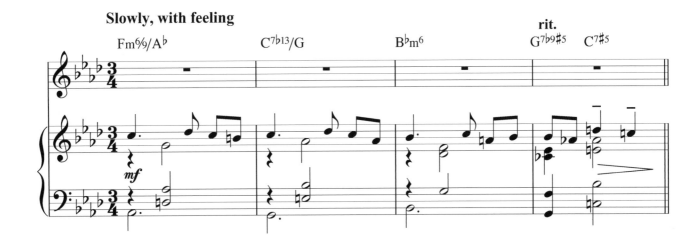

Once up-on a sum-mer-time, just like to-day, we laughed the hap-py af-ter-noon a-

-way, and stole a kiss in ev-'ry street ca - fé.

You were sweet-ter than the blos-soms on the tree. I was as

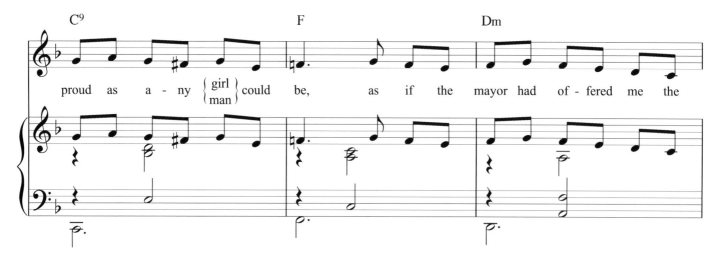

proud as a-ny { girl / man } could be, as if the may-or had of-fered me the

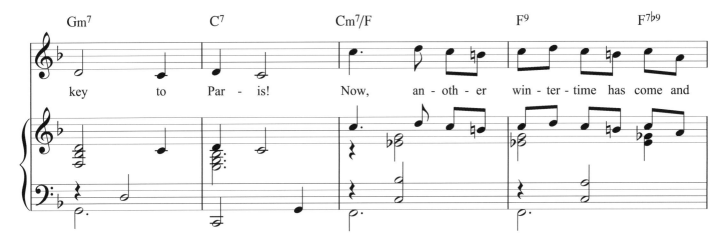

key to Par - is! Now, an - oth - er win - ter - time has come and

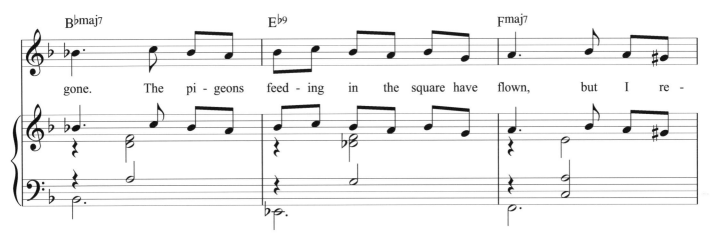

gone. The pi - geons feed - ing in the square have flown, but I re -

- mem - ber when the ves - pers chime. You loved me once up - on a sum - mer -

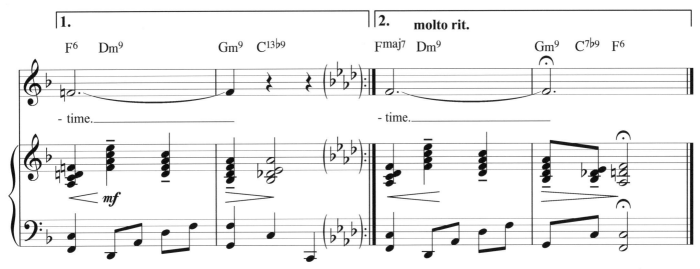

- time. - time.

One At A Time

Music by Michel Legrand
Lyrics by Alan & Marilyn Bergman

Slowly

One___ at a time,___ let me have one

smile___ at a time.___ Give me just one kiss___ at a time___ so we'll have e -

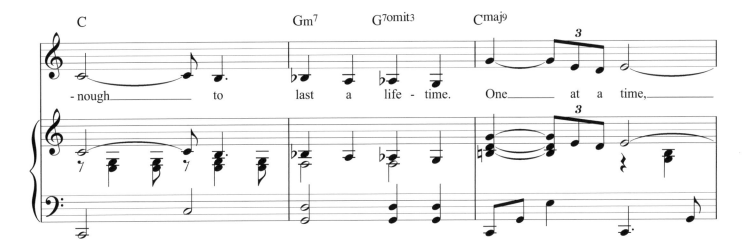

mine___ ev-'ry day;_____ on-ly fools would will___ it a-way, or

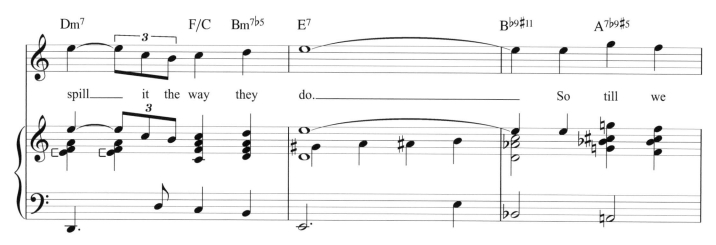

spill___ it the way they do._____ So till we

run___ out of time, give me one___ at a time with you.

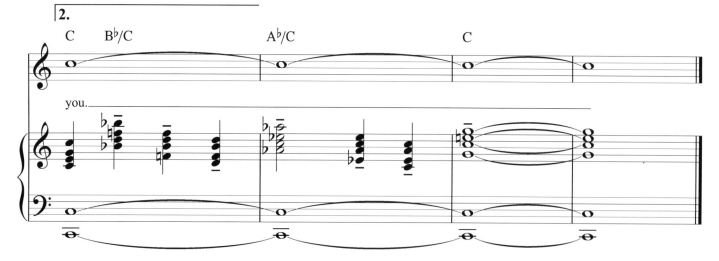

you.___

Barbara Streisand in *Yentl* (1983). UNITED ARTISTS

Papa, Can You Hear Me?

from *Yentl (1983)*

Words by Alan & Marilyn Bergman
Music by Michel Legrand

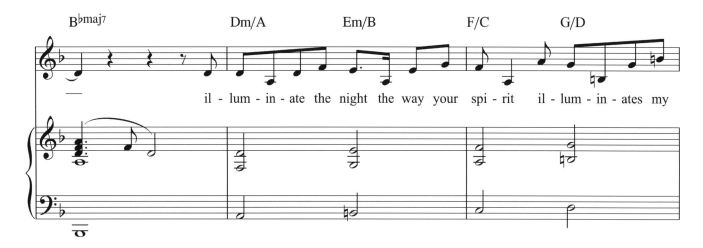

63

Rubato

Pa - pa, how I love you! Pa - pa, how I need you! Pa - pa how I miss you

kiss - ing me good - night.

Verse 2:

Papa, please forgive me
Try to understand me
Papa, don't you know I had no choice?
Can you hear me praying?
Anything I'm saying?
Even though the night is filled with voices?
I remember everything you taught me,
Every book I've ever read.
Can all the words in all the books
Help me to face what lies ahead?
The trees are so much taller,
And I feel so much smaller,
The moon is twice as lonely
And the stars are half as bright.

Secret Places

from *Secret Places (1984)*

Words & Music by Michel Legrand

Moderately

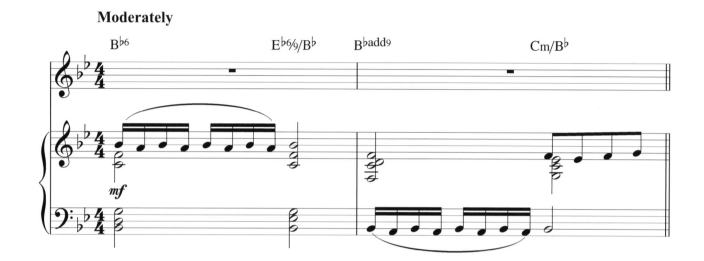

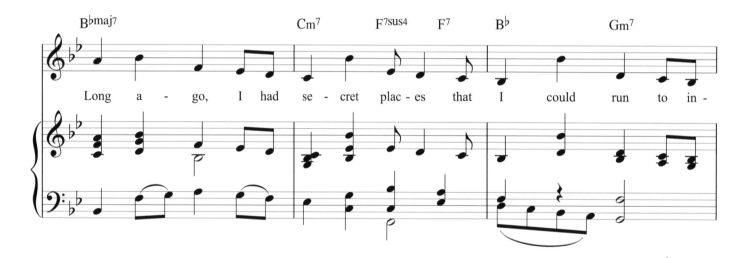

Long a - go, I had se - cret plac - es that I could run to in -

- side me. There were sun - filled hill - tops a - blaze with flow - ers,

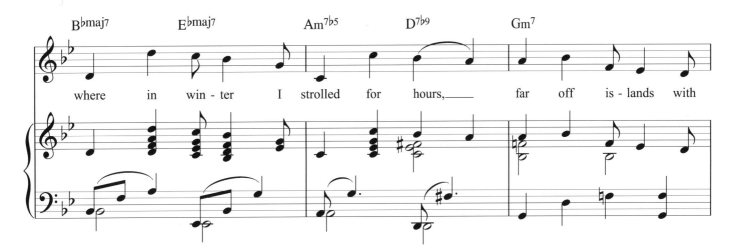

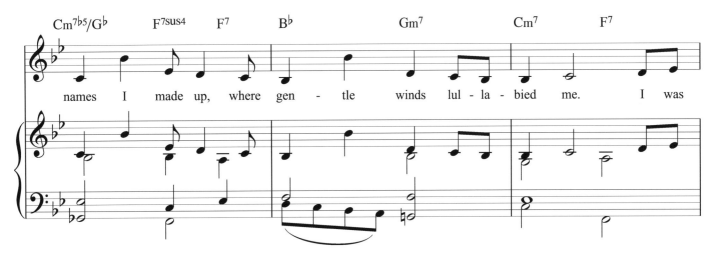

fall - ing mist of time. And now I search each day, but I've

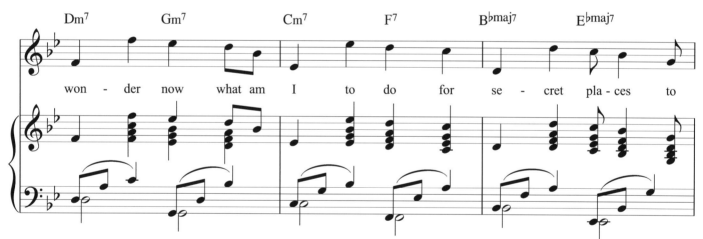

lost my way, lost the child who once used to guide me. And I

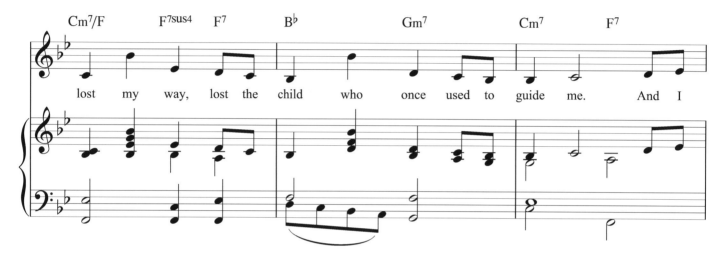

won - der now what am I to do for se - cret pla - ces to

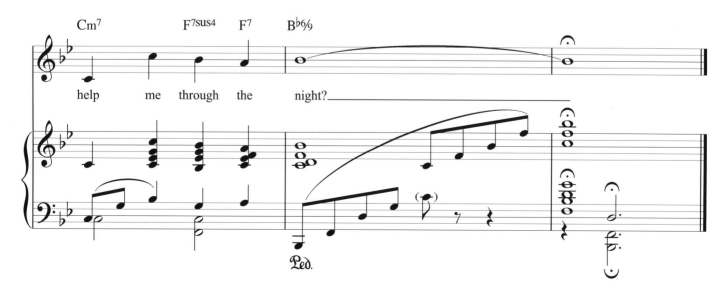

help me through the night?

Sweet Gingerbread Man

Words by Alan & Marilyn Bergman
Music by Michel Legrand

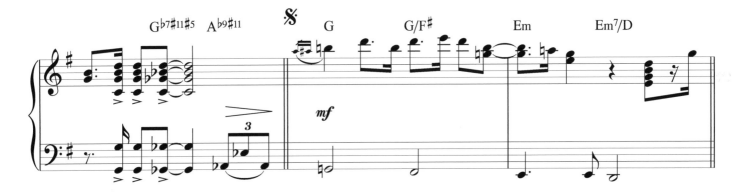

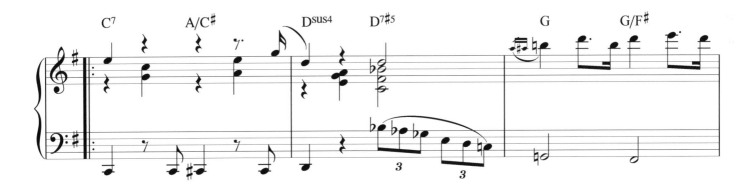

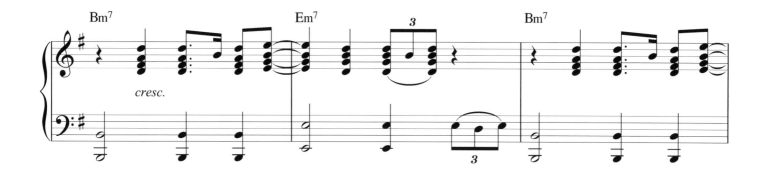

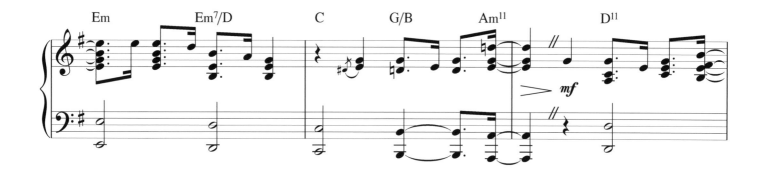

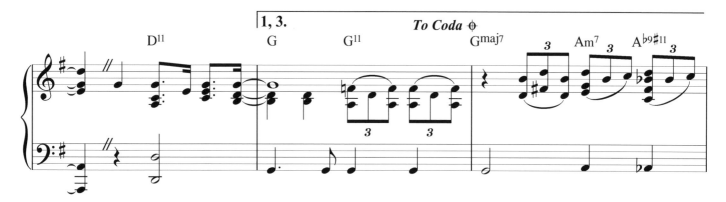

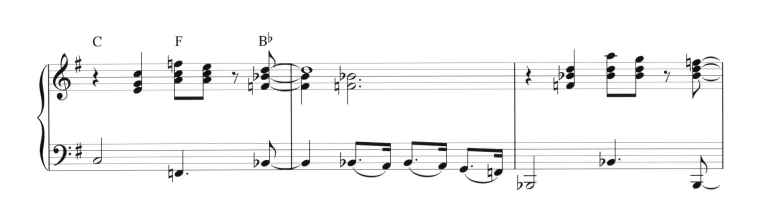

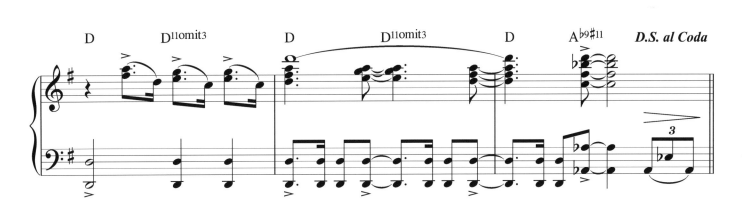

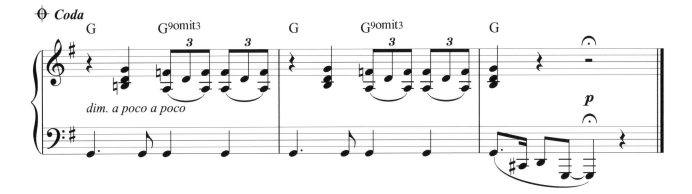

Tell A Lie

Words & Music by Michel Legrand & Marshall Barer

Ballad, ad lib.

Tell a lie, start with just a ti-ny

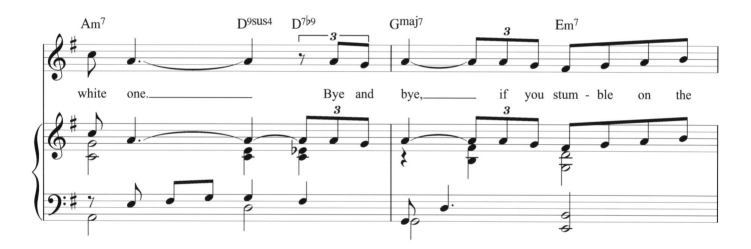

white one.____ Bye and bye,____ if you stum-ble on the

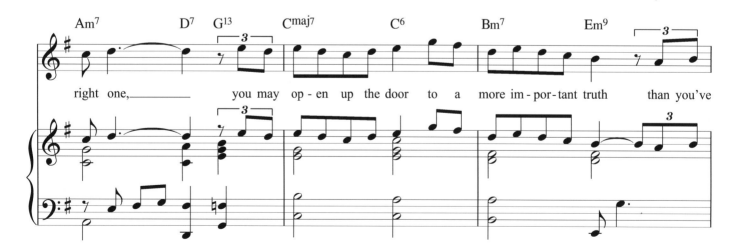

right one,____ you may op-en up the door to a more im-por-tant truth than you've

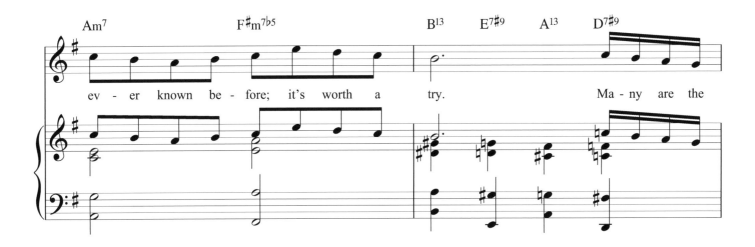

ev - er known be - fore; it's worth a try.   Ma - ny are the

means,_____ for the hope - ful heart's ful - fill - ing,_____ cer - tain

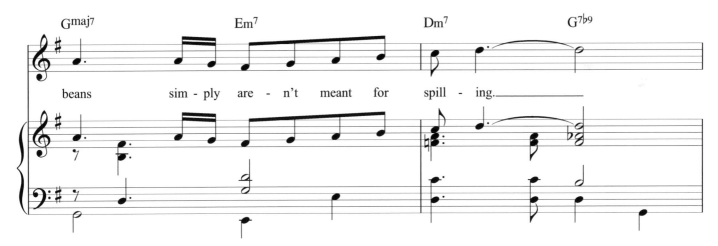

beans   sim - ply are - n't meant for spill - ing._____

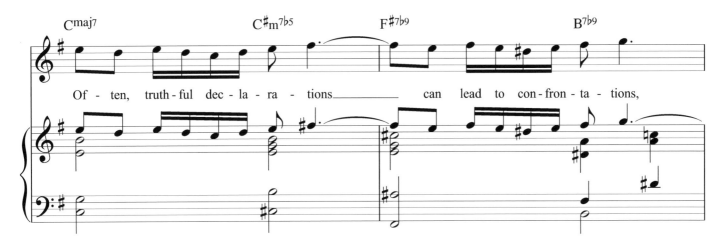

Of - ten, truth - ful dec - la - ra - tions_____ can lead to con - fron - ta - tions,

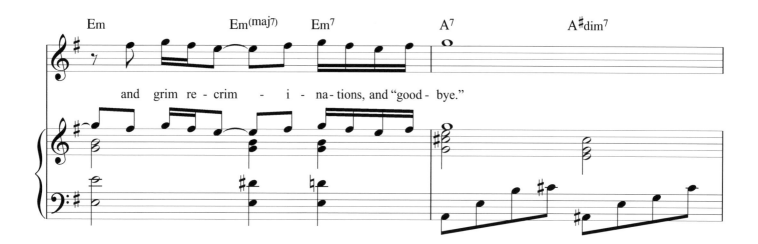

and grim re-crim - i - na-tions, and "good - bye."

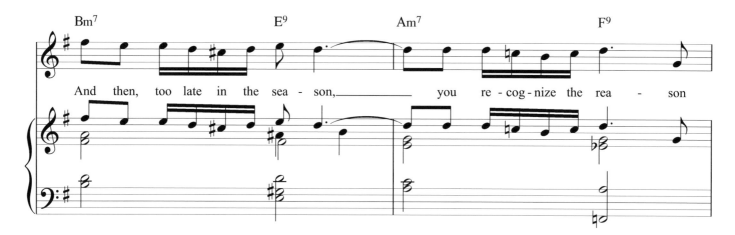

And then, too late in the sea - son,_____ you re-cog-nize the rea - son

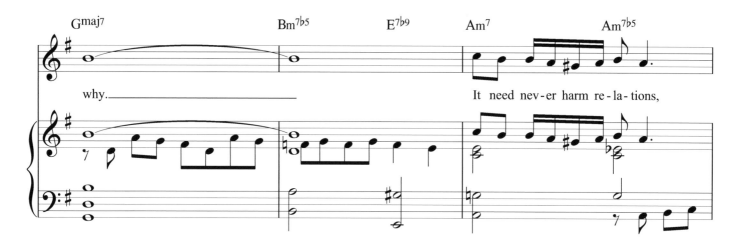

why._____ It need nev-er harm re-la-tions,

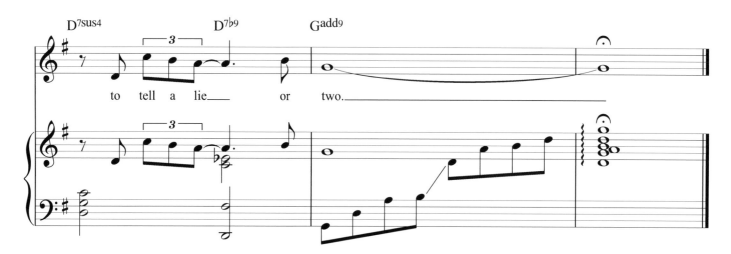

to tell a lie___ or two._____

74

Waiting

from *Marguerite*

Music by Michel Legrand
Lyrics by Alain Boublil & Herbert Kretzmer

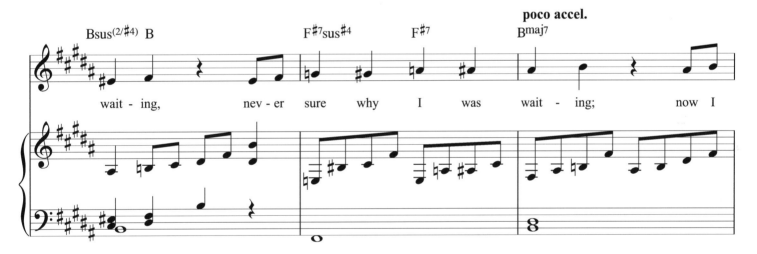

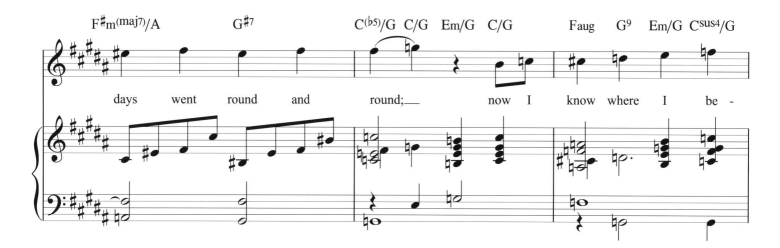

days went round and round;___ now I know where I be -

- long,___ now I see a dif - ferent way,___ now I hear a diff -'rent

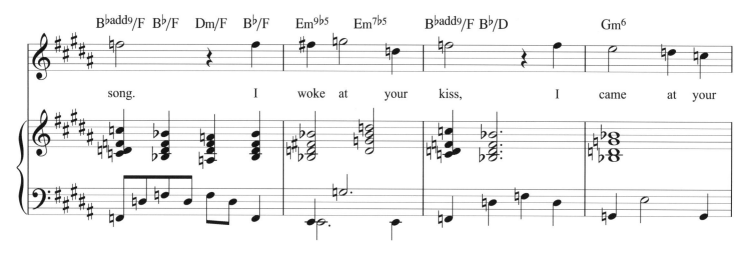

song. I woke at your kiss, I came at your

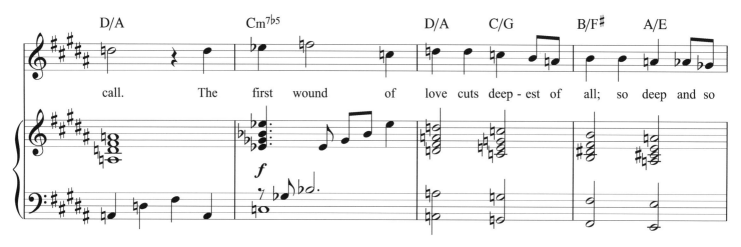

call. The first wound of love cuts deep - est of all; so deep and so

77

Watch What Happens

Words by Norman Gimbel
Music by Michel Legrand

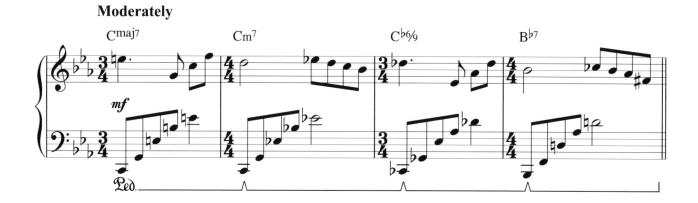

Let some-one start be-liev-ing in you, let him hold out his

hand. Let him touch you and watch what hap - pens.

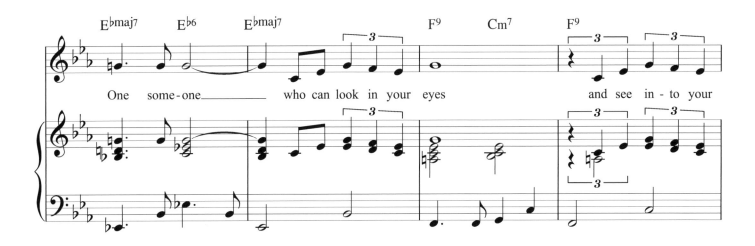

One some-one_____ who can look in your eyes and see in - to your

heart. Let him find you and watch what hap - pens.

Cold, no, I won't be - lieve your heart is cold,_____ may - be

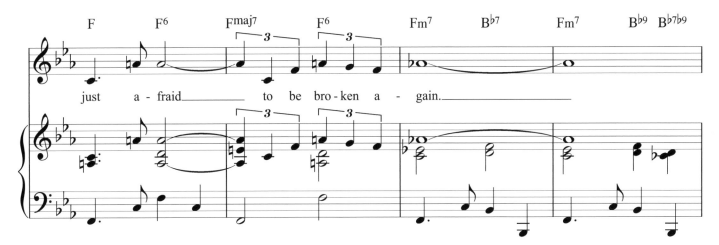

just a - fraid_____ to be bro - ken a - gain._____

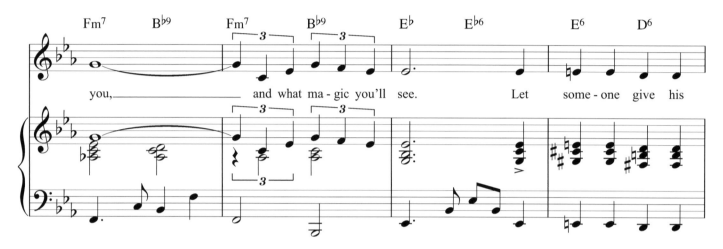

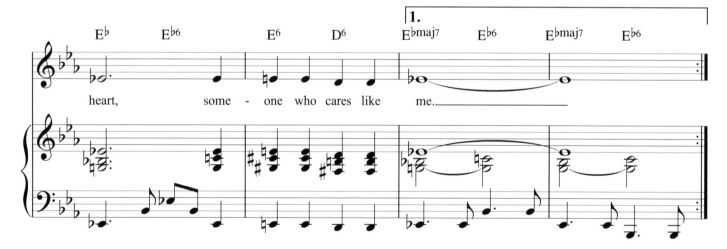

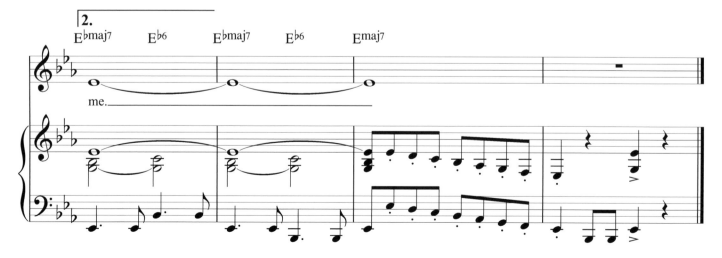

The Happy Ending (1969). UNITED ARTISTS/GETTY IMAGES

What Are You Doing The Rest Of Your Life?

from *The Happy Ending (1969)*

Words by Alan & Marilyn Bergman
Music by Michel Legrand

Moderately with feeling

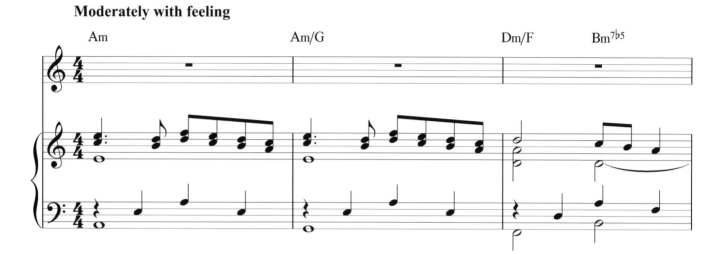

What are you do-ing the rest of your life?_____ North and south and east and

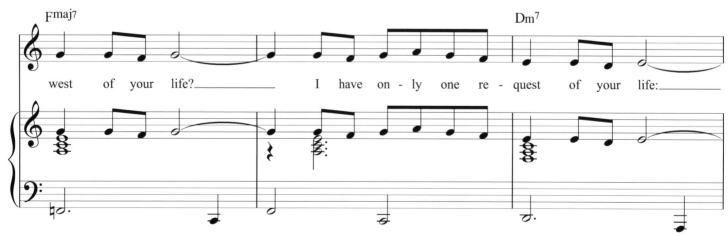

west of your life?_____ I have on-ly one re-quest of your life:_____

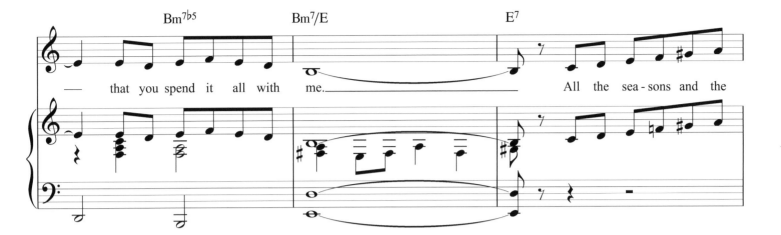

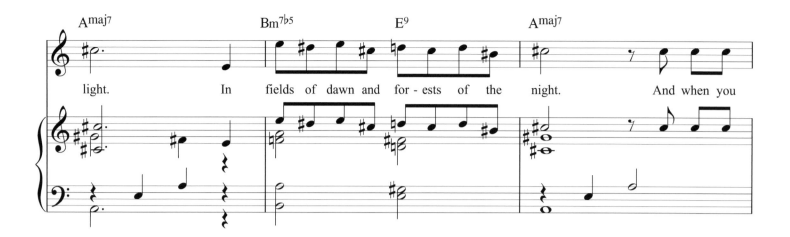

light.   In   fields of dawn and for-ests of the   night.   And when you

stand be-fore the can-dles on a   cake,   oh, let me be the   one to hear the si-lent wish you

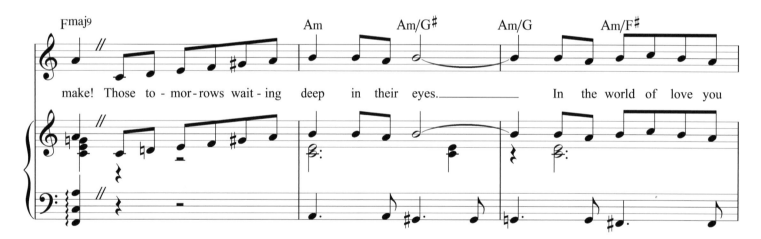

make! Those to-mor-rows wait-ing deep   in their eyes._____   In the world of love you

keep   in your eyes._____   I'll a-wak-en what's a-sleep   in your eyes._____

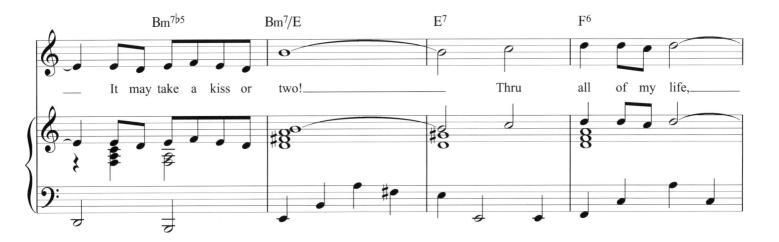

It may take a kiss or two!_____ Thru all of my life,_____

sum - mer, win - ter, spring and fall of my life._____ All I ev - er will re -

-call of my life is all of my life with you!

What are you do - ing the you!_____

The Windmills Of Your Mind

from *The Thomas Crown Affair (1968)*

Words by Alan & Marilyn Bergman
Music by Michel Legrand

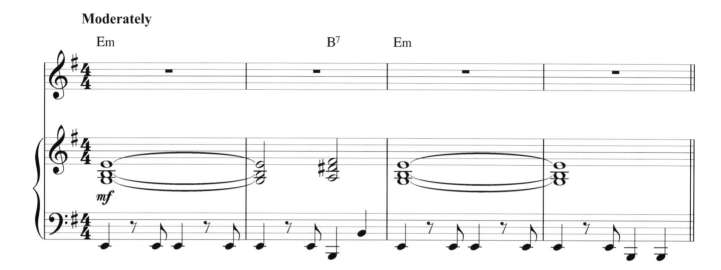

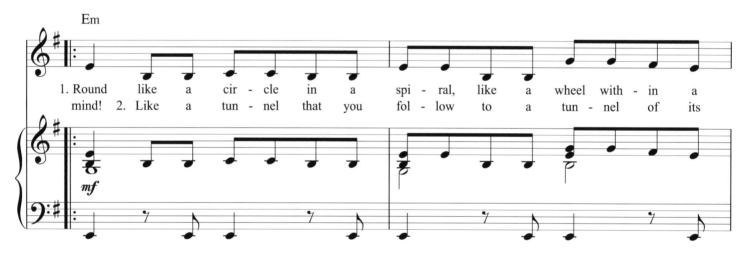

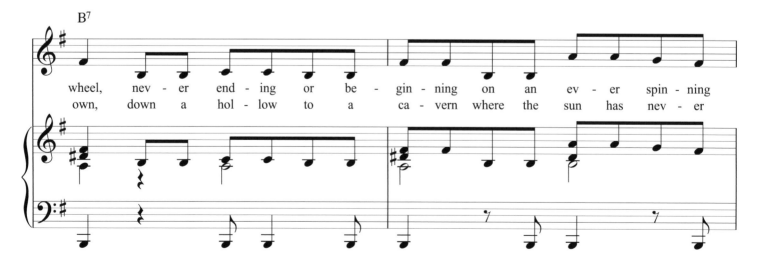

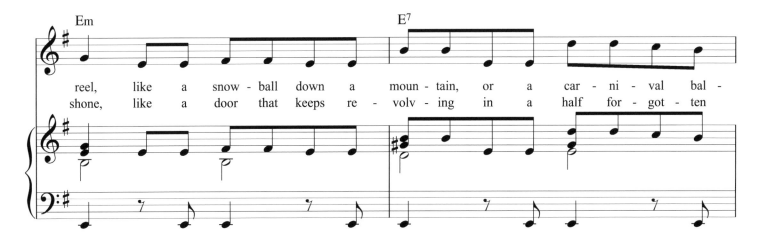

reel, like a snow-ball down a moun-tain, or a car-ni-val bal-
shone, like a door that keeps re-volv-ing in a half for-got-ten

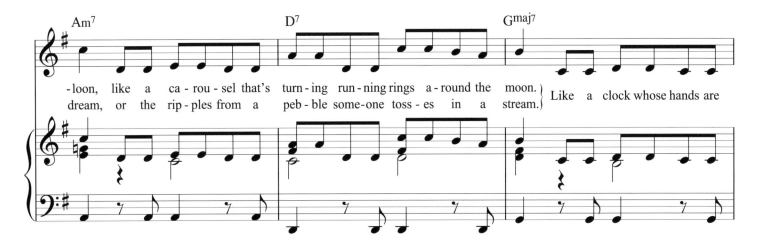

-loon, like a ca-rou-sel that's turn-ing run-ning rings a-round the moon.
dream, or the rip-ples from a peb-ble some-one toss-es in a stream. } Like a clock whose hands are

sweep-ing past the min-utes of its face, and the world is like an ap-ple whirl-ing si-lent-ly in

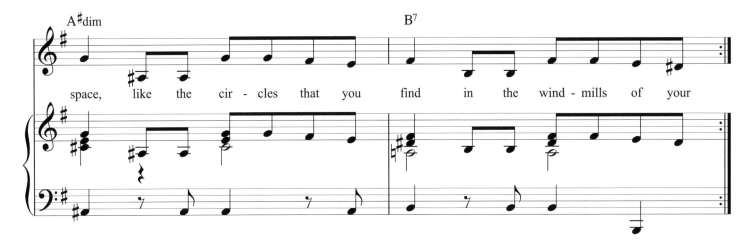

space, like the cir-cles that you find in the wind-mills of your

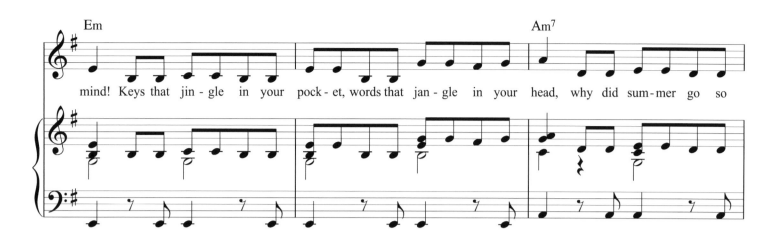

mind! Keys that jin - gle in your pock - et, words that jan - gle in your head, why did sum - mer go so

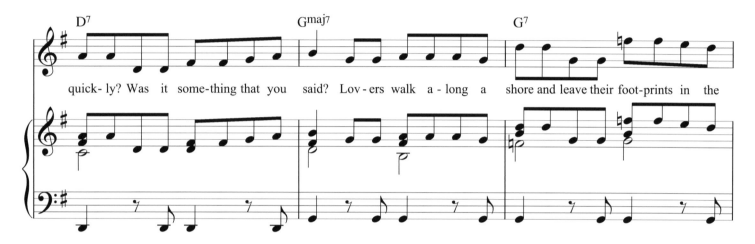

quick - ly? Was it some-thing that you said? Lov - ers walk a - long a shore and leave their foot-prints in the

sand, is the sound of dis - tant drum-ming just the fin - gers of your hand? Pic-tures hang-ing in a

hall-way and the frag-ment of a song. Half re - mem-bered names and fa - ces but to whom do they be -

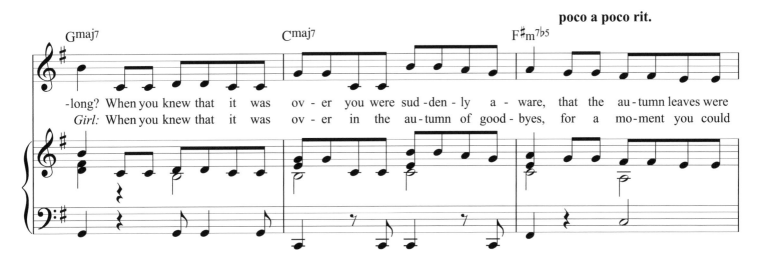

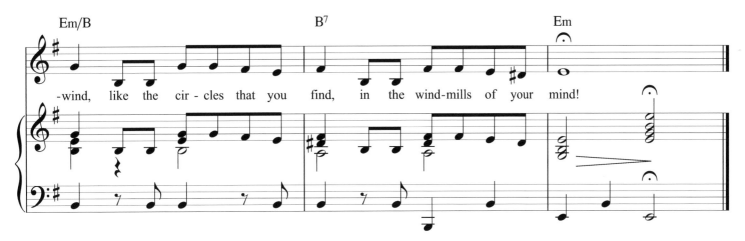

The Years Of My Youth

Words by Hal Shaper
Music by Michel Legrand

Moderately slow, with expression

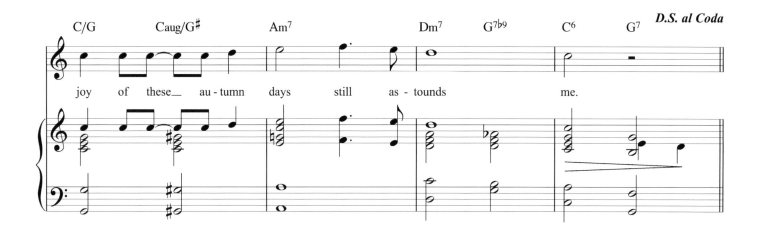

joy of these— au-tumn days still as-tounds me.

Coda

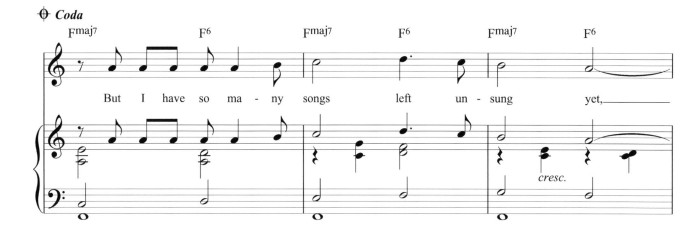

But I have so ma-ny songs left un-sung yet,_____

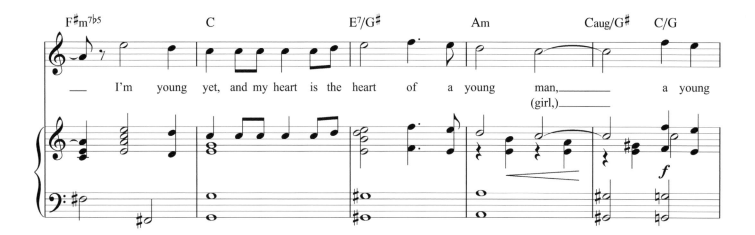

_____ I'm young yet, and my heart is the heart of a young man,_____ a young
(girl,)_____

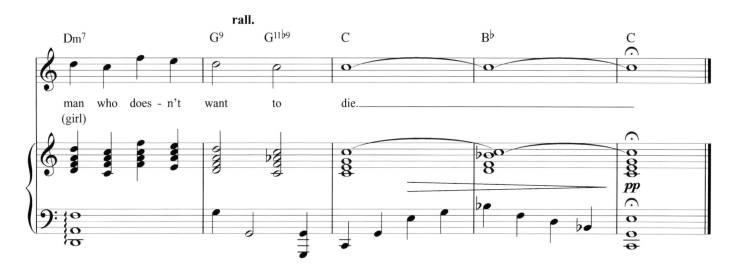

man who does-n't want to die._____
(girl)

You Must Believe In Spring

Words by Alan Bergman, Marilyn Bergman & Jacques Demy
Music by Michel Legrand

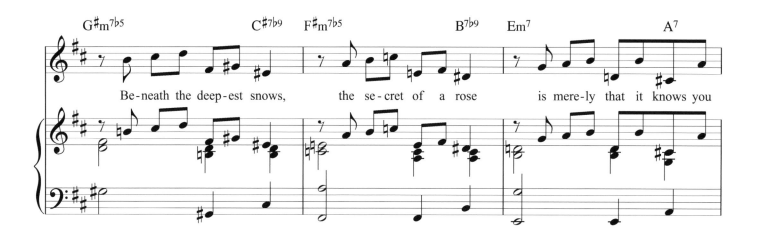

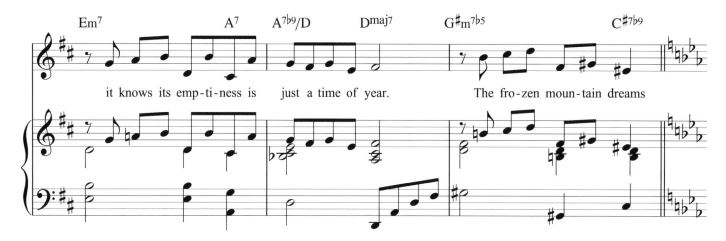

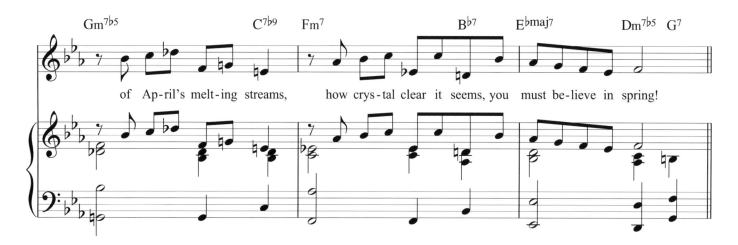

You must be-lieve in love and trust it's on its way,

just as the sleep-ing rose a - waits the kiss of May. So in a world of snow,

of things that come and go, where what you think you know, you

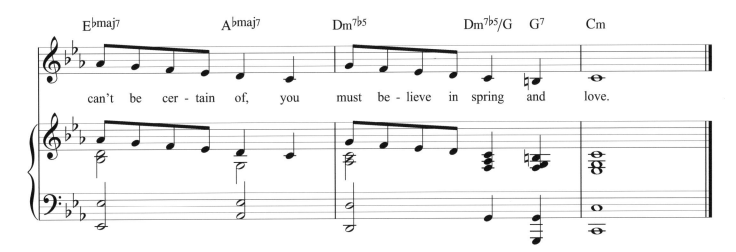

can't be cer - tain of, you must be-lieve in spring and love.